Hereng!
Can't wait to
your book! Write it!
-Ashlu

Lessons I Found

in the Laundry

Basket

Lessons I Found in the Laundry Basket

How to lose the *dirt* and find *joy* and *purpose* in motherhood.

Ashlee Kasten

XULON PRESS

Xulon Press
2301 Lucien Way #415
Maitland, FL 32751
407.339.4217
www.xulonpress.com

Printed in the United States of America.

ISBN-13: 978-1-5456-7965-4

To my husband who always supports my dreams and makes me feel like the most loved woman in the world—Thank you for always being in my cheering corner. I love you.

To my three little kittens who made me a mom—You're worth every batch of laundry. I love you to pieces.

To my parents who inspired me to write great books that leave a legacy—Thank you for always believing in me!
I love you.

To my sister who has been alongside me through this whole process—Thank you! I owe you big time!

To all of my mama friends who cheered me on through this entire process—I am more thankful for you than you will ever know.

Contents

Introduction

Hello friend.

I know we may have never met, but yes, I consider you a friend. Why? Because something about this motherhood thing gives us an instant connection, doesn't it?

Take this for example: ever been in the middle of Walmart, and your child is on the floor in full tantrum mode, letting out noises that sound like a mix between a raptor and an asthmatic pig? Meanwhile, you're standing there trying to decide whether you should punish your child first or spray him down with Lysol. Then, in that moment, another sweet mom strolls by with a cart full of children and three half-eaten bags of chips, and she gives you that, "I've been there, girl" look. You have no clue what she binge watches on Netflix, or what her parenting style is, or even what her name is, but suddenly she feels like a friend.

We need each other. God didn't design us to do this alone, and I believe it's time for us to stop judging and belittling one another and start reaching out our hands to pick that struggling mama up and give her a drink of the water she is calling out for.

When God put this book on my heart, a couple of years ago, I had you in mind. I had no clear idea of what God wanted me to write about yet, but my heart was stirring for the weary mom who needed hope.

As I wrote this book, I was blown away by how God began to give me wisdom to share in the middle of the everyday motherhood moments. While I was cooking dinner, teaching the toddler to share, or folding the laundry, God started to pour into my spirit so that I could pour into you.

God wants to do the same for you. He wants to speak to you in the middle of the chaos. He wants to draw you into His heart and give you the clarity, direction, and peace that you need. He wants to take the mundane and turn it into something more fulfilling than you've ever experienced. He wants you to find the lessons in the laundry basket as well.

My prayer for you is that you'll let the words of this book wash over you in the coming days. Let them begin to bring healing, instruction, and a fresh perspective. And above all, let them bring you into His heart, where you will find all you need.

XO,
Ashlee

The Pre-Treat

Like that chocolate-stained dress, sometimes you need a
pre-treat or the wash isn't going to do a darn thing.

Chapter 1

Morning Prayer Time: Where It All Starts

I have a confession. In our house we are professional, yet accidental, co-sleepers. It's not something we ever planned on, but somehow our California King bed has turned into a church camp slumber party. In determination to keep our marriage as the number one priority in the house, my husband and I have always agreed that the kids will at least start off the night in their own beds, but it never fails. Every night, those sneaky, chubby-cheeked, apple-juice-breathed beings that we love so dearly end up horizontal in between us in what we like to call the "H is for hell" position.

My husband and I have agreed we really wouldn't have it any other way, though. We both realize one day these babies will gag at the thought of curling up next to mom and dad in bed, and we'll once again have that California King all to ourselves the whole night long. Oh, think of the space I'll have! (Excuse me as I drift off into a daydream of massive down pillows, white sheets, and the smell of lavender instead of peanut butter.)

With all that being said, there's something that I've learned from having little people in my bed every morning. These little ones wake up with such delight, don't they? It's as if they entered some kind of secret sleep portal where they're filled with caffeine and laughing gas. They wake up ready to play, ready for our attention, and ready for a glorious day. Me, on the other hand, I roll out of bed looking like I was clearly running late and missed the portal, hit two potholes on the way over, had my hair chewed on by a cat, and borrowed gym clothes from a high schooler.

However, even when I feel my worst, something magical happens around six a.m. in my house. You see this is—and has been for quite some time—my quiet prayer and worship time with God in my prayer closet. As I pull myself out of bed and walk to my closet with one eye still closed, I feel my heart start to beat with joy: I know HE is here. I know this is where I will climb in His lap, and He will fill my heart with joy, peace, strength, and a renewed passion for the job that requires so much—mothering these little ones. When I come into my prayer closet, I am instantly transformed into a bright-eyed child, eager to play, eager to be held, eager to just be in His presence.

I'll never forget sitting there one morning on my closet floor, surrounded by shoes and tossed laundry that didn't make it to the hamper; I was given a vision that has stuck with me ever since. I saw myself coming to Jesus with an empty pitcher. As I approached Him, He took His own pitcher and filled mine with water, until it was running over and spilling onto the floor. I turned around, smiling at the outpouring from Jesus, and saw my kids standing behind me with empty pitchers as well. I took what I had and started to fill their pitchers, until each vessel was overflowing just as mine had been. When I was finished pouring, I had plenty left over. I then heard God tell me that if I don't come to Him first thing in the morning, ready to be filled, then I have nothing to give my children. If I miss my morning appointment with Him, I spend my entire day running on empty.

I'll tell you what, it's rare that I miss my appointment after that very clear message!

Does this sound like you, friend? Are you running on empty, trying to fill everyone's pitcher throughout the day? Are you tired of being tired?

This burden will never be lifted until you give it up. So often we walk around life carrying a weight that was never ours to carry. The Bible says in Matthew 11:28-29, "Come to me, all who labor and are heavy laden, and I will give you rest. Take my yoke upon you, and learn from me, for I am gentle and lowly in heart, and you will find rest for your souls."

It's a promise. Make it a priority to go to Jesus every morning, and allow Him to take the weight off your shoulders and fill up your pitcher. It doesn't have to be an hour. It can be five minutes. There are plenty of days where my time is sparse, but can I just tell you: I have seen Him do more with my measly five minutes than I ever could have done with five million minutes on my own.

This book is the beginning of a new life for you. When you start to experience mornings in His presence, you won't want to go back. When you see Him answering your prayers, filling you with peace, changing the atmosphere of your home, and changing your heart, you'll begin to long for your morning time with Jesus.

WHEN YOU SEE HIM ANSWERING YOUR PRAYERS, FILLING YOU WITH PEACE, CHANGING THE ATMOSPHERE OF YOUR HOME, AND CHANGING YOUR HEART, YOU'LL BEGIN TO LONG FOR YOUR MORNING TIME WITH JESUS.

This is what I like to call the "pre-treat." We're about to jump into a heavy-duty cleansing that will change your life, but before we can get into any cleansing, we must first learn to go to Him daily and release everything to Him.

Are you ready? Today is the day. Ask Jesus to help you get in the habit of waking up and giving Him your attention before anything else each morning.

Satisfy us in the morning with your steadfast love, that we may rejoice and be glad all our days. (Psalms 90:14 ESV)

The Wash Cycle

Where the socks and stains disappear. Just jump in, mama.
No sniff-test required.

Chapter 2

Feeling Overwhelmed

What kind of mom are you? Are you the Pinterest-perfect, sparkling clean mom whose underwear drawer is color coordinated and sorted by styles and occasions? Or are you the one whose "underwear drawer" is really just the laundry basket since you rarely actually put the laundry away? If you're the latter, you'll find yourself in good company here.

I have dreams of being organized and my junk drawers—ahem, I mean *drawer*—never being so full that I have to do the jiggle, yank, and pry to get it open.

While I rarely have a clean room in our house, I do try and at least contain most of the clutter and chaos to one specific room of the house; a room only the bravest souls walk barefoot in: the playroom. In this room, you are sure to find at least twenty-seven pairs of Barbie shoes scattered about, fourteen dance costumes inside out on the floor, a gang of baby dolls stripped naked, purses stuffed with cell phones, plastic food, dress-up shoes, and stolen utensils from the kitchen drawer. Why the kitchen utensils always get taken, I'll never know.

Just the other day I asked my girls to go clean up this monstrosity they had created, and I'll never forget the look on my four-year-old's face.

With tears welling up in her eyes, she looked at me and said, "It's just too much mommy!"

Those sweet little words from her trembling lips pierced my soul as I began to feel the Holy Spirit speak to me.

"*It's just too much.*" Have you ever felt like that?

My marriage is too far gone. We barely talk and there's just too much resentment, hurt, and neglect to move forward.

Our finances are too messy. We're in a mountain of debt and my dreams of staying at home will never come true.

The secret I hide is too deep to expose. It will cause too much damage, cost too much to repair, and is better left hidden.

As I stood there looking at the playroom and down at my four-year-old's downcast face, I simply replied, "It's not too much, love. Mommy will help."

Where do you need God's help today? What areas of your life make you tear up or lash out when you are faced with the reality of the mess?

The thing about God is that He's big. Really big. And our huge mountains aren't huge to Him. In fact, they aren't even mountains to Him. To God those are just opportunities for Him to swoop in, shower us in His peace, and prove once again that He is faithful. All we need to do is turn to Him like a child, put up our hands in surrender, and ask for help.

You will find He actually delights in this! If He didn't want us to run to Him, He wouldn't have crafted us with an innate necessity for dependency. We'd be superheroes who could solve every problem ourselves, never casting out a cry for help, never longing for a shoulder to catch our falling tears, and never finding ourselves in circumstances out of our control.

Have you ever heard the saying, "God will never give you anything you can't handle?" As good as it sounds, it simply isn't true. God will often give us more than we can handle, because it forces us to rely on Him to carry the rest of the weight. John 15:4-5 says, "Abide in me, and I in you. As the branch cannot bear fruit by itself, unless it abides in the vine, neither can you, unless you abide in me. I am the vine; you are the branches. Whoever abides in me and I in him, he it is that bears much fruit, for apart from me you can do nothing."

GOD WILL OFTEN GIVE US MORE THAN WE CAN
HANDLE, BECAUSE IT FORCES US TO RELY ON HIM TO
CARRY THE REST OF THE WEIGHT.

All it takes is a cry for relief from a softened heart that is willing to repent and admit, "It's just too much." Ask Jesus today to help you turn to Him with your mess, as you trust Him to carry the full weight of every uncontrollable circumstance, every teardrop, and every call for help.

**Let us then with confidence draw near to the throne of grace,
that we may receive mercy and find grace to help in time of need.
(Hebrews 4:16 ESV)**

Chapter 3

Complaining

One of my favorite times of day in our house is around six o'clock in the evening. This is when our little family of five sits down at the dinner table to share stories and a warm meal. As the main cook in the house, I take pride in my meals. In all honesty, my spaghetti and meatballs and Taco Tuesday ensembles are nothing to write home about, but when I serve something that's warm, includes at least one veggie, and doesn't include a toy with the meal, I think it's worth being proud of.

I would love to say that my sweet little children praise my efforts and shower me in blessings before graciously offering to do the dishes and asking for seconds on veggies, but this is not the picture of our dining room. Usually there's some kind of wince or eyeroll from the seven-year-old on the vegetable of choice, which then signals to the four-year-old that it's time to protest, which in turn signals to the one-year-old that it is indeed time to flip her tray and let mom know what they really think of peas. Naturally, that is dad's cue to over-appreciate mom's efforts and scramble to pull everyone together before mom loses her cool and decrees that every child in the kingdom shall go to bed with no dinner. Anyone been there?

In our house, we use this simple phrase when it comes to mealtime: "It doesn't have to be your favorite, but just don't complain."

What does this mean? It means that it's okay for not everything in life to be rainbows and kittens. Life isn't about receiving our desires in order to gain happiness. It's about desiring to receive happiness in what we've already gained.

One of the biggest examples of this that I can personally share is the joyous task of washing and folding the laundry. I cannot think of any other household chore that I dread more than laundry. (And yet God gave me a book with "laundry" in the title. He certainly does have a sense of humor!)

It's not that I mind emptying the hampers into the washing machine. That part is easy. And transferring it into the dryer is actually quite therapeutic. But something happens as I take the clothes out of the dryer. Suddenly I have no machine to rely on to finish the job, and the thought of folding every single piece of clothing, walking each pile to its designated room, to then be put away in its designated drawer completely overwhelms me. Truth be told, this household task has always stirred up a fiery attitude within my heart, resembling something similar to the attitude of a toddler demanding the "blue cup" instead of the "red cup." Honestly, I may have cursed under my breath a time or two when I found secret piles of clothes slung behind doors or under beds after I finally got to the bottom of the laundry basket.

But here's what broke me.

One day I was scrolling social media, and I stumbled on a post from a friend. She was describing the heartache she and her husband were going through not being able to conceive a child. She shared a picture of a newborn onesie she had bought in hopes that one day a little bundle would fill it.

I couldn't help but feel God tug at my heart and show me how very blessed I was to have mountains of unfolded laundry. You see, I have mountains of laundry because we are a family of five. I am blessed to have met the man of my dreams. It is my honor to wash his laundry for him after a long day of working so hard to provide for our family. I am blessed to have given birth to three beautiful children. It is a joy to be able to watch them grow and care for them while they are little.

Do you see what happens when you choose gratefulness over complaining? Suddenly our perspective changes. We gain a heavenly viewpoint of life on Earth, and our vision is no longer clouded by what we think we need or what we don't have. When we position ourselves in praise, it is then that we are opened to receive the blessings God has for us. Even more: when we fix our eyes on the blessings, we suddenly become a blessing to those around us.

> WHEN WE POSITION OURSELVES IN PRAISE, IT IS THEN
> THAT WE ARE OPENED TO RECEIVE THE BLESSINGS
> GOD HAS FOR US.

We are blessed, friend. Don't block God from pouring out the good gifts He has for you by remaining in a state of grumbling and complaining. God gives us a clear picture of the harm of complaining in the story of the Israelites who delayed the Promised Land because of grumbling and disobedience. God delivers them from bondage and promised to usher them into a land flowing with milk and honey, but they (like my kids) complained the entire car ride there. I love Moses' response in Exodus 16:8: "Your grumbling is not against us but against the Lord." That will make you rethink your next complaint, huh?

Some of the biggest blessings we have yet to see are just around the corner, but we will delay (or miss them altogether) unless we fill our mouths with thanksgiving and resist the urge to complain.

What can you thank God for today in your life? Where do you need His help changing your attitude? Today, ask Him to grant you the vision to see His blessings in the mundane, difficult, or irritating spaces of your life.

Rejoice always, pray continually, give thanks in all circumstances; for this is God's will for you in Christ Jesus. (1 Thessalonians 5:16-18 NIV)

Chapter 4

You're Not Enough

❧

*H*ave you ever completely blown it as a mom? I mean *really* blown it. Made your kids cry because you lost your temper, let them down with an unfulfilled promise, or said things that you later realized may have hurt their little hearts.

My hand is raised.

While I can think of several examples, there's no other incident that made me truly feel my inadequacies like this one. My oldest daughter is somewhat of a strong-willed child. While she is also extremely sweet and loving, when something doesn't go her way she has the impressive ability to take on the human form of part raptor, part T-Rex, with blond hair and a pink bow on top. There was actually a stage of about a year and a half in her life where tantrums in our house looked like something out of a Jurassic Park movie, and I considered running and hiding until they were over. The truth is, I never knew how to handle it. My daughter had always been so compliant up until this point, and I wasn't sure of how to parent in this season.

There was one day in particular when my inadequacies became so painfully obvious. Something trivial had set my daughter off that morning. I cannot even remember what it was—what followed has completely

17

wiped away my memory of the buildup—but it was enough for her to start putting on her armor and readying herself for a cage-fight with mom. I remember her running from me all around the house, laughing at me anytime I told her what her punishment was. I tried it all. Time out, spanking, taking away toys, nothing worked. She was dead set that she was going to win this battle. I became so enraged, so defeated, so hopeless, that I literally opened my front door, walked outside, went out into the front yard and yelled out and cried. I was so enraged and consumed with feelings of inadequacy that this was the only thing I could think to do. At this point, I remember my daughter following me outside and asking what I was doing, to which I replied, "I'm taking a break! Now go back inside." She refused. So I looked her in the eye, walked inside, and shut and locked the door. Yep, I said it. I locked my child outside.

Of course, about ten seconds later I let her inside, but it was enough to shake her up and make her realize that a) mom had just totally gone off her rocker and b) that refusing to come inside probably isn't something to repeat. It wasn't a proud moment for me. She came inside crying and saying, "Why don't you want me?"

I remember the way my stomach ached like I had just taken the blow of a punch, the heaviness on my heart, and the thoughts of regret, shame, and guilt running through my head. I felt like the world's worst mom, clearly unable to parent her in this season and afraid of what the future might hold.

It was in this moment that I felt God wrap His arms around me and show me something that has stuck with me throughout my journey as a mom.

I am not enough so that He can be my everything. It was designed this way.

If anything is absolutely guaranteed as a mom, it is this: we are not enough. Our human nature dictates that we will constantly fall short. We will make mistakes, won't always have the right answers, and are sure to let ourselves and our children down. That's reassuring, isn't it?

But lucky for us, it doesn't end there! We aren't left in our shortcomings without hope.

If the God of the universe designed us knowing we'd end up flawed, rest assured He has a plan for these shortcomings. Chances are good He's going to use these *imperfections* for good and make beauty from our messes. Every area where we see weakness, He is our mighty warrior, swooping in to bring the strength we lack. Every time we royally screw up, He surrounds us in His overwhelming grace and gently brings instruction and guidance.

The Bible tells us in James 3:2: "For we all stumble in many ways. And if anyone does not stumble in what he says, he is a perfect man, able also to bridle his whole body." Did you hear that? For *we all* stumble—but that's why Jesus died, for moms like us who have a hard time controlling our tempers, our tongue, our thoughts, and our actions. He gets to show us His unyielding love in those moments. As Romans 5:8 (NIV) says, "But God demonstrates His own love for us in this: While we were still sinners, Christ died for us."

This, my dear friend, is the very purpose of our holy call to Christ-centered motherhood. It's our job to show our kids not that we're perfect, but how to submit our imperfections to God and rely on Him. It's our job to point them towards their Maker, and teach them about the love He has for us. He didn't wait for us to be perfect to die for us; He did it in the mess.

IT'S OUR JOB TO SHOW OUR KIDS NOT THAT WE'RE
PERFECT, BUT HOW TO SUBMIT OUR IMPERFECTIONS
TO GOD AND RELY ON HIM.

Let Him show you His strength in your weakness today, mama! As you approach His throne, allow Him to immerse you in the grace you desperately need, draw you towards His heart, and embrace you in the Father's love, which enables you to see the work He's doing with your imperfections. Let Him be enough.

But he said to me, "My grace is sufficient for you, for my power is made perfect in weakness." Therefore I will boast all the more gladly of my weaknesses, so that the power of Christ may rest upon me. (2 Corinthians 12:9 ESV)

Chapter 5

Comparison

*H*ave you ever been on a playdate you had high hopes for that left you feeling a little, umm, inadequate?

About a year ago, my kids were invited over to an acquaintance's house for a playdate. This particular mom and I had really hit it off when we first met, and we were eager to get our kids together as well. It was like blind-dating, but for kids, and the ultimate test for our new, budding friendship. This playdate would determine whether or not we could, in fact, be best mom-friends; the kind of friends whose kids would play for hours together without fighting while we sipped LaCroix on the back porch and talked marriage, friendships, and faith. I have a feeling you've been on this date too.

From the moment we arrived, this mother was nothing short of amazing. She offered us drinks, fed us lunch, and even set up games for the kids in the backyard! What made it even better was that our girls were having a blast together. This date could not have been going better. In fact, I was almost positive there was going to be a second playdate!

However, as the morning went on, I noticed something that instantly made me begin to question our compatibility. Her house was completely spotless. Totally clean. Not a spot of dirt anywhere. Her books were organized alphabetically. Her girls had their own rooms, which were kept cleaner than an operating room. Her husband's office looked like something out of a presidential museum, where everything sat perfectly in its spot, untouched. And as we all ate and played, she continually tidied up behind us, never sitting down to rest. Literally. *Never...*

So I did what any mom does after a heartbreaking first playdate: I went home, ate a gallon of ice cream, and cried over the fact that my new friend would never accept me after she saw the pile of Goldfish crumbs and crayons on the floor of my minivan.

Just kidding. I didn't do that. But I really did sit and wonder if I would ever be able to truly let her in and be completely myself around this gem of a woman. And the poor dear didn't do anything wrong. In fact, she did everything right!

The reason I didn't feel like I could allow that sweet mama into my inner circle of friends is because of one simple factor that had nothing to do with her and everything to do with me. The one simple factor that kills all joy on contact–comparison. I looked at her spotless floors that you could literally eat off of, her sink that was clear of that morning's breakfast dishes, and her lack of laundry baskets lying all over the couch and I told myself that I was lesser. I told myself that we couldn't become close friends because she would judge me. I would never be able to have her over to my house because I'd have to call in a cleaning crew first!

I almost robbed myself of a beautiful friendship that day, and simultaneously almost robbed myself of joy. It never ceases to amaze me how quickly we start comparing ourselves to others and cutting ourselves short. We see the petite mom with a baby on her hip in designer shorts with her flawless, tan legs at the park and immediately, without any prompting or hesitation, we cut ourselves down, build a wall as big as Russia, and run to the other side of the playground where we don't have to look at Ms. Skinny Legs. Or what happens when our mom-friend throws a birthday party for her child, and we arrive to a bar-beque that feels more like a wedding, complete with handwritten cards, handmade paper flowers, and personalized goodie bags with your child's name embroidered on them? We tell ourselves our princess party pack bought straight from Aisle Three at Target is worthless.

We have to stop this game. We will never win. Comparison kills joy every single time. Joy will always be stifled.

How do we stop this torturous ritual? We start with repentance. You see, when we play the comparison game, we are ultimately telling the Father He didn't do His job properly: "You didn't make me more detail-oriented. You didn't give me a beautiful singing voice. You didn't give me an extroverted personality. You didn't make me a prized possession, you simply made me ordinary." Can you hear the enemy's voice in all those words?

The second thing we need to do is allow God to sweetly remind us of who He says we are and what He sees in us. His word tells us in Psalm 139:13-16:

> For you formed my inward parts; you knitted me together in my mother's womb. I praise you, for I am fearfully and wonderfully made. Wonderful are your works; my soul knows it very well. My frame was not hidden from you, when I was being made in secret, intricately woven in the depths of the earth. Your eyes saw my unformed substance; in your book were written, every one of them, the days that were formed for me, when as yet there was none of them.

All the beautiful, varied aspects of who you are were carefully knitted together before you were even a thought in your mother's head. You are far too magnificent and extraordinary to ever compare to anyone else. There will never, in the entire existence of the world, be another you.

YOU ARE FAR TOO MAGNIFICENT AND
EXTRAORDINARY TO EVER COMPARE TO ANYONE ELSE.
THERE WILL NEVER, IN THE ENTIRE EXISTENCE OF THE
WORLD, BE ANOTHER YOU.

Today do this one thing. Sit down with Jesus and ask Him to show you three things He's gifted you with. Your smile. Your sense of humor. Your talent in the kitchen. Ask Him to show you His favorite qualities, talents, or traits. Then write them down.

Whenever you fall victim to another game of comparison, reread Psalm 139:13-16 and go back to that list of who Jesus says you are, because you, friend, were carefully crafted by the extraordinary Father, and He is incapable of making anything "ordinary."

But now, O Lord, you are our Father; we are the clay, and you are our potter; we are all the work of your hand. (Isaiah 64:8 ESV)

Chapter 6

Loneliness

*I*t's three p.m. and my house is a wreck. My sink is full of dirty dishes, my kids feasted on cookies for lunch, and my laundry pile is way past the point of neglect—but my heart! Oh, my heart is so full.

Here in the midst of a scene of complete and total chaos, in which no one should possibly feel at peace, encouraged, or overjoyed, I am totally filled up and thanking God for His goodness. Why? Because I opened my un-scrubbed, fingerprint-besmirched doors and invited in a friend who always fills my heart with joy, and whose children I love like my own.

How often do you open your doors and allow the company of cherished friends to flood the rooms of your home? Do you extend warm invitations of conversation and fellowship to the moms around you, where upon arriving, you sit and share your hearts amongst the laundry and Legos scattered all over the floor?

If you're like me, it's not nearly often enough. I frequently find myself entirely overwhelmed by the state of my house. This alone, often keeps me from even considering hosting a playdate or moms' night. I examine the disastrous mess and am exhausted simply thinking about what it would take to get it to look halfway decent.

Not to mention, there's all those unfinished projects! I can't possibly have anyone over until the fixtures have been replaced in the halfway remodeled bathroom!

If it's not the state of my house, then it's the state of my heart. I'm stuck in my feelings of isolation, being overwhelmed, tired, or frustrated, but instead of reaching out to a lifeline whom I trust with my heart, I withdraw and drown in my pool of self-pity.

Ever been there?

When I was a first-time mom, I remember feeling very isolated. I had just left my teaching career to become a stay-at-home mom, and while I absolutely loved my time with my daughter, I was left feeling overworked, underappreciated, and desperate for human interaction. During this time, another sweet, young mother began inviting me over to her house. It wasn't anything fancy or even planned out. Her house was never perfect. She never had a huge spread of snacks for us. And there were plenty of unfinished projects around her house that could have easily bothered her enough to keep me out—but she didn't.

While this friend may have just assumed our playdates were nothing more than a small mark on my calendar, she had no idea what they were doing to my heart. These unscheduled, imperfect, raw playdates began to breathe life into me. Every time we were together, she would make us a cup of tea and we would sit on her couch and pour out our hearts. We confessed fears that limited us in our capabilities as moms, cried over milestones that made us painfully aware that our babies were growing up, and laughed uncontrollably as we exchanged stories of parenting fails. She would also take the time to ask meaningful, deep questions, and she quickly became my first mommy "heart-friend."

Many of us feel the tug of isolation at our backs in our daily grind of motherhood. We believe the guilt we feel, the exhaustion we wear, or the tantrums we face are uncommon. We believe the lies that no one would understand what we feel, that no one loses their temper like we do, or that no one neglects their marriage like we have.

This, my friend, is why we need each other. We were created for relationships. The impetus was at the very beginning of human creation when God skillfully crafted a partner for Adam. God never intended for us to be isolated. He created us to encourage one another, sharpen each other, and bestow hospitality and kindness that bubbles up from the love He pours out to us. Proverbs 27:9 says, "Oil and perfume make the heart glad; and the sweetness of a friend comes from his earnest counsel."

GOD NEVER INTENDED FOR US TO BE ISOLATED. HE CREATED US TO ENCOURAGE ONE ANOTHER, SHARPEN EACH OTHER, AND BESTOW HOSPITALITY AND KINDNESS THAT BUBBLES UP FROM THE LOVE HE POURS OUT TO US.

If I can encourage you in one thing today, it's this: do not let the days, weeks, months pass by without allowing yourself to experience the sweetness of a friend's counsel. Don't let the busyness of your day, the condition of your house, or whatever other excuse you can find keep you from opening your door to a God-given breath of fresh air. You will find that as you do, you will grow in your walk with God and in your role as a mom.

Many times, I hear moms complain that they would love to have those deep connections, but they just don't have any moms around them to connect with. Maybe that's true. In that case, it's time to start praying friends in; ask, with expectancy, for God to plant the right people in your life that will flourish into cherished friends with time and effort.

I'd also like to gently suggest that perhaps you—and the majority of us—do in fact have these friends within reach, but may have simply neglected to nurture these blessings and allow them to become heart connections. We want others to befriend us, but we often aren't willing to be the first to initiate the friendship. I urge you to look around and identify the moms who inspire you, encourage you, walk with the Lord, and whose children you want yours to befriend. Then pursue them. Open your doors. Invite them in. Make them a cup of tea. You just might find that on the other side, there is a mom who is finally taking a deep breath as well and who is leaving with her heart overflowing from your companionship.

Today, ask God to show you the future "heart-friends" He's placed in your life and ask Him for the bravery to begin to pursue those relationships. If you don't have other moms in your life, ask Him to begin to gather them around you, to give you creative ideas on how to actively seek them out, and to stir up the faith within you to keep believing that He desires for you to be in relationships, even when it feels hopeless.

So whatever you wish that others would do to you, do also to them, for this is the Law and the Prophets. (Matthew 7:12 ESV)

Chapter 7

Balancing It All

If there is one hour of the day that is almost always guaranteed to be, ahem, should I say, adventurous, it's the hour between starting to cook dinner and dinner being on the table. It's during this hour that my "momming" skills are always tested to the limit. How much can you handle at once, mom? We're about to find out.

Here's how this hour usually plays out. I head into the kitchen to prep, and the one-year-old follows behind, begging for me to pick her up. So I sling her on my hip and begin the one-handed egg crack, which I'm thinking is probably the most valuable thing I learned in my high school culinary classes. I put her back down on the floor as I chop the vegetables, at which point she starts unearthing and eating three-day-old cereal pieces and raisins that escaped under the table. Okay. Back up she goes.

As I'm cooking, I get a text reminding me to pay for this year's home-school group. Also, that reminds me, I need to pay the mortgage. I'm sure I can do that really fast while cooking. It's at this moment my four-year-old comes in and announces she's so hungry she cannot possibly wait for dinner. After reassuring her she will not starve, while simultaneously fastening the baby into her high chair with a tray of rice puffs, my middle child throws herself on the floor and tells me it's not fair that I let the baby feast while she is clearly being neglected.

Cue the seven-year-old to need my assistance getting down her paint set, finding her pajamas, or heaven forbid, unclogging the toilet. This will continue for a solid hour and at the end of this, you can be assured: my floor will be covered in rice puffs, the four-year-old will have been in timeout at least once for yelling, and I will be forcing a smile on my face as my husband walks through the door, excited to talk about his day and our weekend plans.

Balance.

Can you relate? I'm sure you can.

One of the most challenging jobs we have as moms is keeping our lives in balance. A dear friend of mine said it best when she was venting her feelings of being overwhelmed: "You know, if you're doing amazing at one thing, you can be sure you're failing at everything else." That might be a bit of an exaggeration, but I can't say I haven't felt this to be true at times!

Ever feel that way? This week you're an amazing mom. You're attentive, creative, present, and patient. However, your business has been neglected, the house is a wreck, and you're pretty sure your friends have disowned you for not responding to a single text message.

I've got good news, friend. It doesn't have to be this way.

We live in a society that pushes for one thing: performance.

Do better. Be better. Volunteer more. Serve your community. Put your kids in multiple sports. Have the biggest following on social media. Make the best meals. Earn more money.

It's exhausting and completely contradictory to the way we were created. It wasn't God who created us to be over-burdened performance seekers; we did that on our own. We've fed the lie that in order to be accepted, successful, and happy, we need to prove our worth through our acts; to do more and be more. He clearly demolished this lie when He gave the ultimate gift of love on the cross. The crucifixion and new life in Christ was not a reward for our impressive earthly performances. Ephesians 2:8-9 backs it up: "For by grace you have been saved through faith. And this is not your own doing; it is the gift of God, not a result of works, so that no one may boast."

WE'VE FED THE LIE THAT IN ORDER TO BE ACCEPTED, SUCCESSFUL, AND HAPPY, WE NEED TO PROVE OUR WORTH THROUGH OUR ACTS; TO DO MORE AND BE MORE.

We often tell ourselves that if we could only (fill in the blank) that we'd be a better mom, a better wife, or a happier person. Armed with this lie, we justify filling our schedule with just *one* more activity...often to find that one extra commitment tips the scale and sends us into a whirlwind of busyness, stress, and resentment.

How do we get off the crazy train? We start by balancing ourselves. A wagon with a missing wheel can't carry any weight, and the same is true for you.

Invite Jesus into your day to be this missing wheel by giving Him your time first thing in the morning. Without this, you can guarantee everything else will be out of balance. Ask Him to show you where things have gotten out of balance, what areas of neglect need your attention, and what commitments you've made that aren't in His will for you.

Here's what I've found most helpful as I've sifted through my life, seeking this balance. Spend time praying, and make a list of four things God has put on your heart for your family. Is it missions? Homeschooling? Spending quality time together, investing in your marriage, or eating family dinner together? Four things. Take those four focal points, and post them on your fridge. When you start your day, look at that list and ask yourself how your schedule aligns with those four priorities. When you're asked by others to commit to another project, ask yourself if it fits into your four. This might mean you start saying no to a lot, but it also means you get to start saying yes to a whole lot more that *matters* to you, and your joy and peace will increase as a result.

As you begin to identify activities, commitments, and tasks that don't support one of your priorities, you will notice that when you choose to add their weight to your plate, you feel stressed, busy, and unfulfilled. Start your day with resting in the fact that you don't need to be excellent at everything, sweet mother. You are already excellent because you were crafted by a Creator who doesn't make anything just ordinary.

Today, focus on the things He's laid on your heart and lay that which is unnecessary to the side. Ask God to reveal areas inhabiting your spirit that are draining, damaging, or gratuitous. Do this simple thing so that your heart is free to find more joy than you've ever imagined.

Do not be conformed to this world, but be transformed by the renewal of your mind, that by testing you may discern what is the will of God, what is good and acceptable and perfect. (Romans 12:2 ESV)

Chapter 8

Taming Our Tongue

*H*ave you ever constructed something beautiful? Something brilliant and unique? Or do you remember, as a child, coming to your parents with artwork in hand, beaming all over, excited to show them your family portrait you drew with your new pack of Crayolas?

Though I have never been much of an artist (my girls tell me my drawings of people look more like snow monsters with claws), I still get that feeling of pride after creating something, whether it's painting a piece of furniture or cooking a dinner that involves more than three ingredients. There's just something built in me—in us—that delights in seeing a finished project. A piece of our heart bursts with pride when we've used our hands, skills, or minds to bring forth beauty.

When my girls want to get crafty during our homeschool day, I usually end up pulling out a box of crayons or markers and a half-used notebook and calling it "art class." It's just not my gift. However, there is one thing I absolutely love to do with them during this time, and that's creating sculptures with Play-Doh. Okay, "sculptures" makes it sound really elaborate. Let me clarify. They're elementary-level models of cats whose heads are so much larger than their bodies they won't even stay attached. Of course, there's also the classic snake and snail shell, because who can really mess up a rolled-out snake?

During this time of molding and sculpting, I'm so mindful of each move I make. Every time I push my fingers into the dough, I leave an imprint. Sometimes the imprint is exactly what I meant for it to be, adding to the beauty of the finished project and further forming it into the master-piece I envision. Other times, I push too hard, move without thinking first, or just lose sight of the end goal and I'm left with an unsightly mess.

Sound a little like parenting?

I remember walking through the halls of our church one Sunday morning. I was in the middle of that hard season with our oldest daughter that I mentioned. She was beginning to show her strong will, and I was drained and in need of water for my weary soul. My mind was being attacked left and right with lies from the enemy of her being ruined for life. My pastor's wife happened to be walking through the hallway at the same moment and stopped to ask how we were doing. When I opened up about her misbehavior and how it was affecting me, she looked at me and uttered words that glued themselves to the inside of my mama-heart for life. She said, "You know, Ashlee, God's going to use that will for His glory. Praise God for it. It may seem hard now, and it's hard to see past it, but know that He put that will in her for a reason. It's your job to mold it. Speak it over her."

Our children are the clay. God is the creator. Our words are the molding tools.

How often do we react to a negative situation without a keen eye focused in on the finished product, reminding ourselves that the best is yet to come for this sweet little soul? Do we snap at our children in a rushed moment trying to get out the door, yell at them as we demand peace and quiet for the fifteenth time in an hour, or use our words as weapons to make them feel the guilt of their wrongdoings? Or perhaps even worse, do we speak about our children as if their God-given strengths were a disability? In speaking about the tongue, James 3:9-10 says, "With it we bless our Lord and Father, and with it we curse people who are made in the likeness of God. From the same mouth come blessing and cursing."

A five-year-old girl is labeled "bossy" by her teachers. Is she? Or is she a future leader who is still in the molding phase?

A two-year-old is frequently silenced and told he's too noisy. What if he's a future Grammy-nominated musician who hears music in everything he does?

Now don't get the wrong message here: I'm not saying that we allow our kids to misbehave, or run without boundaries. Remember, we are the ones designed to mold them, and it's our job to "train them up in the way they should go" (Prov. 22:6). However, we need to have one ear to Heaven listening for His direction in how to parent them.

If we ask God to show us who our children are created to be and what strengths He's given them, He will. Then, just like a precise sculptor, we can carefully choose our words to mold these little people into something beautiful. We can choose not to use words like rebellious, bossy, rude, aggressive, trouble-maker, stubborn, cry-baby, etc., and instead replace them with words from Heaven like leader, gifted, anointed, determined, fearless, compassionate, and more.

JUST LIKE A PRECISE SCULPTOR, WE CAN CAREFULLY CHOOSE OUR WORDS TO MOLD THESE LITTLE PEOPLE INTO SOMETHING BEAUTIFUL.

Today, ask God who these little humans are that He's placed in your care. Who will they be in ten, fifteen, thirty years? Start today with praying that God would break the words you spoke over them in the past, and then move forward as you begin rewriting their destiny, covering them in words of life.

Death and life are in the power of the tongue, and those who love it will eat its fruits. (Proverbs 18:21 ESV)

Chapter 9

Exhaustion

When was the last time you had a newborn in your home? Maybe it's been years for you, but you still remember the long days and long nights of caring for a baby. Or maybe you're nursing one in your arms right now as you read this book, desperate for some down time.

If you've ever had an infant, then I guarantee you've been asked this one question: "Are you getting any sleep?" And if you've had that question asked of you, then you've probably also experienced the sleep-deprived tiger rising within you, throwing your shoe back at the asker with, "What do you think?!" in a hormonal, exhausted meltdown. No? Just me?

I honestly can't count the number of times I've snapped at someone, usually my husband, simply because I was completely rundown and exhausted.

The truth is that as moms, we're just tired. Can I get an amen?

Even long past the newborn stage, we're still drained. We're dizzied from spinning circles while wiping noses and caring for sick kids. We're fatigued from the amount of questions our curious six-year-old asks us all day. We're practically narcoleptic from the amount of laundry— seriously, *the amount of laundry*—that lines the hallway, waiting to be folded. Or maybe it's waiting to be sorted. I don't even remember. Wash it all again.

A few years ago, I heard a pastor being interviewed about his life as a child. He was speaking specifically about his mother and how much he adored her. He talked of how much influence she's had on his life. He was asked by the interviewer what it was specifically he loved most. His answer gripped my heart. He said, "She always had time for me. No matter what she was doing, if I came to her with a question or asked her to play, she would always drop everything and give me her attention."

Feel free to pour yourself a glass of pity party after reading that. I did.

Just kidding! Let me tell you, friend, I think there are only a few, rare, maybe-they're-fictional moms who can honestly say they fit this description. It's quite possible his recollection of his mom excludes any of the times she did have to say "just a minute." However, there is still much to be gleaned from this.

By nature, we often operate in "do" mode. Clean. Cook. Organize. Shop. Fold. Wipe. Drive. Feed. Dress. For many of us, we lack an off button. There's no sitting and enjoying our children. There's just no time for that! Resting in God's presence? What's that? Sitting on the front porch with a book in hand, filling up your spirit? Ha!

And then we sit and wonder why we feel so overwhelmed, exhausted, unfulfilled, and just simply drained.

Let me ask you something: if the God of the universe, the Alpha and Omega, the all-powerful Lion of Judah, the Great I Am, stopped after creating the universe to do absolutely nothing else but just *rest*, why do we think we are exempt? Why do we think resting is something to feel guilty about, that we can survive without it, or that it's a foolish use of our time?

How often do our kids come and ask us to sit with them while they color, or read a book to them, or watch their performance, and we answer back "just a minute!" Or do you ever feel the pull to begin your morning in prayer, interceding for your family and getting your heart aligned with God's but keep putting it off because there are other things that need to be done around the house?

Rest.

It isn't a luxury. It's a necessity, and God desires for us to have it. Psalm 127:2 says, "It is in vain that you rise up early and go late to rest, eating the bread of anxious toil; for he gives to his beloved sleep."

REST. IT ISN'T A LUXURY. IT'S A NECESSITY, AND GOD
DESIRES FOR US TO HAVE IT.

We need to restfully lean in during time with our kids, just enjoying their presence. Rest time to sincerely listen to what they have to say. Rest for our spirits in prayer time with God. And, of course, physical rest to allow our bodies to heal and refresh.

Here's what we've started in our house as a reminder to me to take time to stop the "doing" and just be present. I've given my kids permission to request five minutes. Five minutes of my time for whatever it is they want. My cuddle-bug always requests a "five-minute hold," while my oldest likes for me to color with her for five minutes.

Let your kids decide what they want your time and attention for, but do them this huge favor: be in a state of rest when you give it to them. I don't mean get out your yoga mat and do the squatting dog, warrior hawk pose. (Can you tell I don't work out?) I mean let your mind be at a state of rest. Put down your phone and forget your to-do list. *Do not* under any circumstances look at the graveyard of sippy cups under their bed, or you'll be cringing at the thought of what might be in them and fighting the urge to start cleaning. Just be there. Watch their little face light up as you interact with them, converse with them, and give them your best.

Then do this favor for yourself: give yourself a five-minute break. Five minutes in the morning with Jesus. Five minutes after the kids go to bed to sit in silence and stare at a wall. Whatever and whenever you can work it in, but allow yourself to hit pause on the constant pull of duties and obligations. Pause and rest; you've earned it, mama.

Today ask God to bless you with the ability to rest. Ask Him to help you see past all the distractions, avoid being a slave to your to-do list, and to gently nudge you when it's time to sit down and listen.

Come to me, all who labor and are heavy laden, and I will give you rest. (Matthew 11:28 ESV)

Chapter 10

Mommy Guilt

⌒⌒

When my kids were younger, I was a part of a mom's group with our church. Every month we'd gather together to listen to an encouraging speaker, eat food, and then we'd chat about that week's topic. These precious meetings were a breath of fresh air. As we would spend time together, it never failed that at some point we'd move to deeper conversations, strengthening our connections and baring our souls. Hearing each other's stories, discovering we were all battling the same battles, and realizing that we were all facing the same fears was uniting. It was rare we'd have a meeting where one (or all) of us weren't sitting in a pile of tears, finally divulging whatever struggle we'd been holding in for months. The more tears, the better the meeting was. It brought such hope, strength, and encouragement to my new mama-heart.

In my recollections of these meetings, I can't specifically recall the struggles of each mother, but I can generally summarize them all with a single word: guilt.

If I just would've been more patient when the toddler was screaming for attention today. If I just would've listened more carefully to my five-year-old's story at bedtime instead of rushing them to sleep. If I just wouldn't have lost my temper when my ten-year-old broke that glass. If I could just work less. If I could just be present more. If I would just smile more and yell less...if I just.

Three words that take away far more than they ever give.

These three words are the ones we continually swirl around in our mind at night as we lay there trying to fall asleep. It's these words that enter our hearts and minds, sweeping through every corner, robbing us of any and every glimmer of joy. Guilt is like that crazy ex-boyfriend from high school. You know, the one you never should have dated in the first place who seemed to show up everywhere you were? The guy who made you nauseous the moment you saw him, and always managed to ruin your night. Craig? Andrew? What was his name again? Yeah. Just like him.

GUILT IS LIKE THAT CRAZY EX-BOYFRIEND FROM HIGH SCHOOL. YOU KNOW, THE ONE YOU NEVER SHOULD HAVE DATED IN THE FIRST PLACE.

You know what really angers me about guilt? He knows no boundaries and leaves no one alone. You try to escape him, but as soon as you fulfill your "if I just," guilt changes the satisfaction goal. He moves the target on you like a cruel game of hide and seek. You work less hours now, but you find yourself saying, "If I just didn't spend so much time cleaning the house instead of playing with my kids."

You know something, my dear friend? Guilt may be like that crazy ex who follows you around trying to ruin your plans, but you have the authority to shut and lock the door. You have the authority from God to refuse to allow the enemy to keep you in a place of depression, regret, shame, and inadequacy. How? Through grace and redemption.

Do you know how much the God of the universe loves you? Do you know how long He spent forming you in His perfect image? Do you know that He specifically chose your children for you, and you alone?

So if the God of the universe created tiny beings to put in your care, knowing very well what flaws and shortcomings you have, don't you think He also provided enough grace to redeem your failures?

The problem with our battle with guilt is that we make it all about us. We make it solely about our performance and what we could have done better. It's not about you, friend. It's about your partnership with a Holy God to parent these precious children and raise them to love Him and fear Him. Remember, God is always there to redeem the situations where we massively mess up. He's always there to wrap us in His grace and show us who He created us to be. Hebrews 4:16 (NIV) says, "Let us then approach God's throne of grace with confidence, so that we may receive mercy and find grace to help us in our time of need."

Now, does this mean we continue wrongful actions under the covering of grace? Absolutely not. It means we allow God to mold us, sharpen us, lead us to repentance, and call us to greater levels in Him, but we also allow Him to come in and heal our own hearts with His abounding grace. Even while He was aware of every failure on the horizon, He still chose you for those precious babies.

Want to know how to end the battle with guilt? Hand the keys of parenting back over to the master, and ask Him to show you where He's sweeping in to save the day as you're falling apart. Right now, ask God to remind you of who He says you are and what He sees in you, and declare those truths over yourself in place of the lies.

Blessed be the God and Father of our Lord Jesus Christ, who has blessed us in Christ with every spiritual blessing in the heavenly places, even as he chose us in him before the foundation of the world, that we should be holy and blameless before him. (Ephesians 1:3-4 ESV)

Chapter 11

Behavior Challenges

*S*ay it with me friends: "Mirror, mirror on the wall, who's that tantrum-ing on the floor at the mall?"

Oh. That's my daughter? Excuse me while I join her.

Here's a fun law of science for you. Children will always throw fits at the most inopportune moment, in the most embarrassing place, with the most amount of people watching. Proven science.

Case in point: one evening my husband and I, along with our two children, were at Disney World. We were there with another couple we are great friends with and their two children. It was getting late and we were just about to leave the park, but I told my oldest daughter we needed to stop at the restroom first before getting in the car just to be sure she didn't have to go. Per usual, she was quick to assure me she absolutely did not need to go, but I knew her better and quickly scooped her up to walk her to the bathroom to try.

Okay, pause for a moment. If this were a movie, it would be at this point that the music dramatically changes from a carefree medley to a suspenseful score indicating impending doom. The child's eyes would mutate to bright red and people around her would start screaming and running in fear.

I don't even remember everything that happened over the next twenty minutes. I'm pretty sure I blacked out.

I do, however, remember my dear friend coming into the bathroom to check on me, assessing the situation, and then turning around and walking out, knowing there was no way in heaven or hell that she was going to be able to do anything to calm this storm. I still refer to it as "The Meltdown of 2014."

The only thing I do remember clearly is how I felt coming out of that bathroom. I looked at my friend and didn't even know what to say. I for sure felt like I was standing in the middle of Disney World, but completely stripped down to my underwear with the stark realization that everyone now knows I wear lacy thongs. It was totally humiliating, and I immediately interpreted the situation as a direct reflection upon my parenting skills.

To be honest, there was more going on behind the scenes that led up to this moment of mom shame. Until this point my child had always been pretty darn close to perfect. People always commented on how well-behaved she was and what a good job I was doing with her. I, of course, thoroughly enjoyed hearing these statements and because of this guilty pleasure, I began to do something very dangerous. I began to think that somehow her sweet, obedient nature was a reflection of my amazing parenting and that she would never be the child who acted out because I was doing such a great job of being a perfect mom.

Well that got shot out of the sky real fast that day.

As parents it's so easy to see our children as a reflection of ourselves. It's easy to see their strengths, successes, and personalities as part of their genetic makeup and upbringing. On the flip-side, it's easy to see their flaws, setbacks, and failures as a reflection upon what we've done or are doing wrong.

Here's where we've got it all wrong though; the Bible doesn't state, "God created man in man's image." And thank God for that! He created man in *His* image. So to think that our children are created to be a reflection of us at all is a self-driven thought.

As humans, it's so easy for us to become self-focused. It's our world, our homes, our families, our children. We have to remember that despite our greatest efforts and our grand gestures, at the end of the day our children are created to be a complete reflection of Jesus. Even on the day they're tantrum-ing. Even on the day they graduate college with honors. They are His. We are but mere tools used to polish the masterpiece He has created them to be. You see, we are all created to be masterpieces that reflect our King. However, because we live in a world of sin, we need to continually be sharpened, molded, stripped down, and refined.

When our children act out, we think, "Where have I gone wrong in parenting?" Really, we should be thinking, "How does God want to use me to mold their spirit and polish their character so they reflect Him more?"

You might think of it this way: when a painter begins working on a masterpiece, do onlookers stop him in the middle of his progress and say, "Well looks like you majorly screwed this one up!" Or, "Clearly you aren't equipped for this." You would never expect a painter's creation to be complete until he puts his paintbrush down.

The same is true with our children. The same is true with us.

To look at our children and say "Clearly I've done something wrong here," is like putting down your paintbrush in the middle of the creation.

TO LOOK AT OUR CHILDREN AND SAY, "CLEARLY I'VE DONE SOMETHING COMPLETELY WRONG HERE" IS LIKE PUTTING DOWN YOUR PAINTBRUSH IN THE MIDDLE OF THE CREATION.

Kids are going to mess up, melt down, and make us insane some days, and that's okay. It's okay because we know that they are little reflections of Jesus that just need sculpting, every single day. Our job is to use the Holy Spirit as our guide to evaluate and adjust as qualities arise that don't line up with who they were created to be. Proverbs 22:6 says, "Train up a child in the way he should go, even when he is old he will not depart from it."

Bottom line, mama, your kids' mall meltdown is not a reflection of your parenting. You're a great mom. The tantrum is just part of the sin-nature we were all born with. Your job is to point this out and direct your little one's eyes back to repentance and redemption.

So go ahead and let the onlookers roll their eyes as your toddler screams and throws a bag of goldfish at the grocery bagger's head, leaving you with no choice but to leave all your groceries on the conveyor belt to go outside for a little "character polishing." You just look them in the eye and tell them you'll be back in five when your kid looks a little more like Jesus.

When do you notice that you take your children's difficult seasons as a reflection of yourself? How can God's word help remove this weight from your shoulders? Ask God to show you His plan for your children and how you can cultivate the strengths He's given them.

Then God said, "Let us make man in our image, after our like-ness. And let them have dominion over the fish of the sea and over the birds of the heavens and over the livestock and over all the earth and over every creeping thing that creeps on the earth." (Genesis 1:26 ESV)

Chapter 12

Losing Yourself

M y husband and I recently celebrated our nine-year wedding anniversary. On this day, in a sentimental moment, I decided to go back and look through our wedding photos and relive the day. I quickly found I couldn't even enjoy looking at them without staring at the "former me" in every photo and envying her perfect arms, tiny waist, and freedom to dance the night away without tiny humans spilling grape juice on her white dress or pulling down her sweetheart top, revealing her perfectly perky self to the entire crowd.

Nowadays, my "perfectly perkies" are defiantly droopy, my tiny waist is rounded and wrinkled, and my freedom is defined to the five minutes a day I get alone as I hide in the cupboard and eat chocolate. It's a far cry from that young, vivacious, twenty-three-year-old girl with the meticulously bobby-pinned updo and the daring, bright pink stilettos.

As I drift off into green-colored visions of what was, I find myself wondering, "Where has she gone and will I ever see her again?" Looking in the mirror is often a similar experience for many of us. We grab at the skin that now droops over our jeans and pull it back, imagining ourselves twenty pounds lighter. Or we watch our friends with no children go on adventures, romantic dates, or even to the bathroom by themselves and long for the life they live.

As I sat staring at these photos, I recognized my sour, ungrateful attitude and began to shift my thinking to how good this new life of mine really is. I looked at that bright-eyed version of myself and thought back to my dreams and goals at that point in life. It's easy to think that my mind would have been focused on the next big vacation or my daring career goals, but they were far from that. My biggest dream for myself was always to be a wife and mom. Ever since I was a little girl, I always envisioned myself standing there with my husband's arms around my neck and my children running around at my feet. I wanted to hold my babies on my hips, rock them to sleep at night, and kiss their boo-boos.

I have all of this. I am living my dream life. That twenty-three-year-old girl is here inside of me somewhere jumping up and down with excitement screaming, "Are you kidding me? This is my life?" Yet here I am on the outside rolling my eyes, picking up wet pajamas, sucking in those extra pounds and mumbling, "Are you kidding me? This is my life?"

There is a nasty lie circling our society these days. A lie that causes us to completely miss our purpose, calling, joy, and best self ever. This lie is that we somehow lose ourselves. That the old us is who we really are at the core, and that if we dare stray from that we are simply floating through life as a ghost of our past.

This simply isn't true. We don't lose ourselves at all. What we actually lose is our perspective.

Maybe before children you were skinny, and yes maybe you thought being thin was more important than life itself. But now your body wears the coveted battle scars of bearing children, and those children are more important than life itself.

Maybe you used to have goals of running your own company and traveling the country to teach entrepreneurship. Now you run your household and when you teach your children, your words have an impact that will affect generations to come.

Perspective.

The thought that you have lost yourself is a lie from the enemy designed to keep you in a place of discontentment. You haven't lost yourself at all, dear one. You have become a better, more giving, and more fruitful version of yourself. Your body, your freedom, and your new life is not a ball and chain, it's a gift. A gift that the former you would have opened with extreme delight. You are living out your purpose. Your old plans and goals were good, but they weren't the best, and God always knows what we need more than we do. Jeremiah 29:11 (NIV) says, "For I know the plans I have for you,' declares the Lord, 'Plans to prosper you and not to harm you, plans to give you hope and a future.'"

THE THOUGHT THAT YOU HAVE LOST YOURSELF IS
A LIE FROM THE ENEMY DESIGNED TO KEEP YOU IN A
PLACE OF DISCONTENTMENT.

Now you might be wondering if this means motherhood and being a wife irrevocably deems you are required to give up all freedom, settling into the fact that you will be serving others twenty-four hours a day. Absolutely not! It's important to have outlets, hobbies, and kid-free ventures, as those will help you stay refreshed and give you more appreciation for your job as a mom.

But just remember, you are your best you today, not yesterday.

Have you believed the lie that you have lost yourself in this role as a mother? As you glance in the mirror today, allow God to reset your perspective, so that you may hold His vision of your life.

Many are the plans in a person's heart, but it is the Lord's purpose that prevails. (Proverbs 19:21 NIV)

Chapter 13

Broken Leadership

*H*ave you ever seen negative habits in your children that painfully point to negative habits you have as well?

Negative self-talk, chewing with your mouth open, or maybe letting a four-letter anthem of praise slip when you step on a Lego.

Recently, in the middle of a very busy season of life, my husband and I noticed how much junk our kids consume when we're rushing around and aren't setting boundaries. We do our best to eat very healthy, but I always like to have a few treats in the house for special occasions and rewards; those are of course the items our children reach directly for when they're looking for a snack. After a few months of eating on the fly and indulging, it was clear that something needed to change.

We both agreed it was time to teach our children about self-control when it comes to junk food and making healthy choices for themselves. I had it all planned out. When we got home from church that Sunday, I'd have charts printed out with healthy options for snacks that they could choose from, and a reward system set up for making those choices. However, this was quickly squashed before Sunday even arrived, as my husband greeted my children at breakfast one morning with a donut in hand and a bag of cookies for the car. I followed up his indulgence with a bowl of ice cream at lunch, with full intentions of polishing off the rest of the pint after dinner. Well so much for that idea!

I quickly realized I probably shouldn't be focusing so much on the children, but instead on the adults who lead them!

Here's how God used my and my husband's sugar binge to show me something so necessary for every area in our parenting walk. In order to effectively lead our children, we must first lead ourselves.

IN ORDER TO EFFECTIVELY LEAD OUR CHILDREN, WE
MUST FIRST LEAD OURSELVES.

How do we expect our children to make wise eating decisions when we don't set any boundaries for ourselves? Why do we expect peace and kindness in our home when we daily cut down our spouse with our words and start arguments? How can we blame our children for habits they've picked up by watching us?

If a company has a large turnover rate and poor customer service, do you look at the employees to figure out what's wrong? Absolutely not. You go straight to the top. You sit with the CEO and demand to know who in the world is running this joint!

Vice-versa: when you drive through a Chick-fil-A and the eighteen-year-old boy replies with "my pleasure" after your two-year-old throws a nugget at him and demands more ketchup, you know someone at the top is doing something right.

If the culture of your home isn't what you've always wanted, if the attitudes are far from a Chick-fil-A drive-through, then it's time to take a look at the leadership. You might remember in an earlier chapter that we talked about not blaming ourselves for our children's difficult seasons—and this still remains true—but we are talking more than meltdowns. What I'm talking about are habits that consistently occur across the entire family, creating a culture.

When there is a culture of whining, talking back, disrespect for authority, and bickering, that's when it's time to self-examine and revamp the leadership.

If you lack peace in the house, is it because you're allowing stress to rule the way you treat your family? Or do you allow distractions, obligations, and excessive commitments to pull away from the necessary "family down-time" that rejuvenates everyone?

If your children are constantly bickering, have you looked at the way you talk to your spouse or children? Do you use words that are uplifting, peaceful, and directed towards the problem—not the person?

Let me ask you this: why would an eighteen-year-old boy working a drive through at a fast food restaurant even think to respond with "my pleasure?" Because his manager does it, and his manager's manager does it. There are many companies who strive to provide excellent customer service and train their employees to do so, but when the leadership doesn't abide by those standards, it destroys any hope of a culture of gratitude and joy.

I love this version of Titus 2:1-6 from The Message translation:
"Your job is to speak out on the things that make for solid doctrine. Guide older men into lives of temperance, dignity, and wisdom, into healthy faith, love, and endurance. Guide older women into lives of reverence so they end up as neither gossips nor drunks, but models of goodness. By looking at them, the younger women will

know how to love their husbands and children, be virtuous and pure, keep a good house, be good wives."

Just by watching the older generation, the next generation will know how to conduct themselves and live lives that bear fruit and bring joy and peace. What does this say about our children? It says they are watching. They are learning. They are modeling after us.

Today, ask Jesus to show you where your leadership needs some sharpening. Let Him identify the bad habits and refine your family culture so that you can lead your family in peace and joy.

Shepherd the flock of God that is among you, exercising oversight, not under compulsion, but willingly, as God would have you; not for shameful gain, but eagerly; not domineering over those in your charge, but being examples to the flock.
(1 Peter 5:2-3 ESV)

Chapter 14

Fear

⟨❧⟩

*I*t was midnight, my kids were in bed. I was just getting ready to shut down for the night as well. My husband was working out of town, and I was alone with the kids, and a bit uneasy. I decided the best thing to do would be to just go to sleep, so I didn't stay up listening to every creak and pop while holding a broomstick in my hand. But as we all know, it's a necessity to bring your phone with you to bed and mindlessly scroll through posts before you fall asleep. There I was completely ruining my REM cycles with the white light and looking at what my friends had eaten that day, discovering who was newly pregnant, and watching mindless videos of dogs kissing babies.

Then I stumbled on it: a post from a friend that read, "Everyone needs to watch this! We have to be prepared." My curious mind clicked on the FOX News video.

If you asked me now what that video was about, I would not even be able to tell you. I don't remember what we were supposed to be prepared for, or who it was we were supposed to be afraid of. All I remember was sitting up in my bed with my heart racing, fear swelling up around me, suffocating me like a pair of my high school jeans.

I spent the next half hour wide awake, thinking about all the worst-case scenarios for my life in the coming days. Would we be at war? Would it be safe to go to the mall, the park, or even the grocery store? Logistically, the best thing to do would be to have all our groceries and supplies shipped to our house from now on, and only venture out to visit friends and family.

I wish I was kidding—but this is exactly what fear does. It makes you think irrationally. It cripples your faith and makes you a little, well quite honestly, a little crazy.

Have you ever been there? There have been so many times in my journey through motherhood thus far that I've allowed fear a place in my house. When my firstborn was a toddler, I was constantly afraid of her getting sick. She didn't have a strong immune system at the time, and it seemed like we were living in and out of viruses, one right after the other. Then there was a time when I feared losing a child. I had been following a blogger who was writing in depth about the pain and loss after losing a child, and I carried around a heavy weight from that point on until I finally realized where it had stemmed from. I've also allowed fear at times to limit me personally. I allowed fear to tell me I wasn't a public speaker, a leader, or anything more than a quiet, shy mom sitting in the back row.

I look back at those times in my life and the faith-filled, confident version of myself wants so desperately to shake that young mom and say, "Kick fear out the door! You have so much waiting for you, but you can't move forward with fear as your driver!" However, I also know if I hadn't walked through it, I couldn't be sitting here today writing about it—so for that I am thankful. I am even more thankful for the knowledge and guidance in getting set free from it.

Did you know that "fear not" or "do not be afraid" are mentioned over one hundred times in the Bible? Could it be that these are the biggest blocks to achieving your full potential and living your best life through Christ? I believe God doesn't want us to fear, because He knows that worry and fear do not produce fruit; instead they produce chains and bondage. When we give in to fear, we allow ourselves to be wrapped up in chains that prevent us from advancing His kingdom, following His will, and allowing Him to use us in great and mighty ways.

WHEN WE GIVE IN TO FEAR, WE ALLOW OURSELVES TO
BE WRAPPED UP IN CHAINS THAT PREVENT US FROM
ADVANCING HIS KINGDOM.

In Matthew 6:25-27, the Bible says,

> "Therefore I tell you, do not worry about your life, what you will eat or drink; or about your body, what you will wear. Is not life more than food, and the body more than clothes? Look at the birds of the air; they do not sow or reap or store away in barns, and yet your heavenly Father feeds them. Are you not much more valuable than they? Can any one of you by worrying add a single hour to your life?"

In Psalm 91:9-13 we read this promise:

> "If you say, 'The Lord is my refuge,' and you make the Most High your dwelling, no harm will overtake you, no disaster will come near your tent. For he will command his angels concerning you to guard you in all your ways; they will lift you up in their hands, so that you will not strike your foot against a stone. You will tread on the lion and the cobra; you will trample the great lion and the serpent."

Does this give you peace? It certainly does to me. Does this guarantee that our life will be perfect? No, but it guarantees that the God who loves us deeply is guarding our lives and protecting us from harm outside of His will. It means that we can let go of fear and begin to trust our Maker and Protector.

So how do we release fear? We release fear by first identifying the roots where fear first took hold. Maybe it was something you walked through that left scars and you fear it will happen again. Maybe like me, it was something you read that caused a spirit of fear to enter your mind. Whatever it is, ask Jesus to help you identify it and release it to Him. Ask Him to show you where He was in that situation, and how He's redeeming it.

I went through this identifying and releasing process with Jesus with a situation that happened to me in middle school. I was at the front of the room giving a speech to my classmates and completely forgot my entire speech halfway through. As I stood there, red-faced and shaking, I heard the snickering and jeering of a boy on the front row. I was mortified. I went back to my seat defeated and afraid to ever get up and speak in front of a crowd again. It took me until thirty years of age to finally identify this root of fear and release it to Jesus. As I revisited that moment, I saw Jesus standing right behind me as I faced the room of students. I saw Him comforting me. Suddenly this wasn't a moment of shame and fear. It was a moment of redemption from a Mighty Savior. It was at that point that I was able to truly break the bondage of fear, give it to Jesus, and move forward in my destiny.

Motherhood is too hard and life is too short to live in the chains of fear. Don't let yourself even move to the next chapter without first handling the fear, my friend. You deserve to live as you were created to live. Free from fear, anxiety, and worry.

Today, let the one who created you be the one who frees you, and make the decision to move forward in confidence, peace, joy, and trust. Then watch what God will do with and through you.

Even though I walk through the valley of the shadow of death, I will fear no evil, for You are with me; your rod and your staff they comfort me. (Psalms 23:4 ESV)

Chapter 15

Self-Pity

〜

*D*o you know anyone who always seems to be in a major crisis and continually complains about how someone did them wrong? When you talk to them, does it seem like they're stuck in a hole of self-pity they can't get out of, or that no matter what you say they will always remain fixed on the negative?

I have met a few of these such individuals in my life, and each time I do, I leave our conversations feeling drained and in need of a bubble bath, a bar of chocolate, and a mindless romantic comedy!

I honestly don't even think these people realize they are such "negative Nancys." I think it's a lifelong pattern they've seen and replicated, and now they don't realize there is any other way. It's like they've identified themselves as a victim, and there's no one who is going to tell them they're not.

As much as I hate to admit it, being the second, sensitive child in my house, I was often this way as a child. Not so much a pessimist, but I took things extremely personally and cried often. I would sit and sulk about situations with friends where I felt left out or mistreated; I retreated and pouted instead of speaking up.

Fast-forward twenty-something years later, and I was beginning to see the same self-pity patterns in my second child. She would cry when the family left the room she was in to another room in the house, yelling, "Everyone just left me!" Or she would whine about having to walk somewhere saying, "My legs are just not strong. I can't walk." Everything was beginning to sound like that familiar song of, "Woe is me. I am the victim."

As you can imagine, this mama was not about to let that fly in our house; for one, whining is just not my love language. You can give me nails on a chalkboard all day long, but send a whining three-year-old in my house and my hair stands on end. Second, I was not willing to watch her develop a "victim mentality" that would stick with her for years. I love her too much to let her prevent herself from moving forward because of the pool of self-pity she was creating.

Before I could address this issue in her, I had to do a self-evaluation of myself. Were there areas in my life where I was still playing the victim or where I lacked confidence and a warrior mentality? How did I act when everyone left their dirty laundry around the house and I was stuck rounding it up, washing it, and putting it all away only to have it strung out again by that evening? How did I respond when my husband called to let me know he had to work late?

I knew the answers to those questions. I could hear myself grumbling and complaining about everyone leaving laundry on the floor for mother to come and pick up. Woe is me. I could hear myself whining when my husband had to work late yet again, telling myself he just didn't understand how hard my job at home was and that I needed the break. Woe is me. It became clear that I still had areas within me where I played that old familiar song in my head, too.

Oh friend, how easily we fall into a trap of self-focused grumbling. Instead of giving thanks and pressing forward in triumphant declarations of truth with the heart of an overcomer, we sit and focus on how hard our situation is. In 1 John 5:4-5 (NIV), the Bible says, "For everyone born of God overcomes the world. This is the victory that has overcome the world, even our faith. Who is it that overcomes the world? Only the one who believes that Jesus is the Son of God."

We are overcomers. We don't have to sit around feeling sorry for ourselves and telling ourselves that we're defeated. We can set our minds on things above, not on earthly things (Col. 3:2). We can ask for a heavenly perspective of who we are, our situation, or our purpose, and begin to declare those truths in place of the self-pity song we used to sing.

What does this look like in our children? It looks like lots of rewriting words and thinking patterns. Where my daughter says, "I can't," we have her say, "I can if I try hard." Where she says "Everyone left me," we have her say, "Everyone is moving and I can choose to follow or stay." We tell her that God made her an overcomer and He clothed her in strength and dignity (Prov. 31:25).

There's no place for self-pity and lies about unworthiness or crippled abilities when you flood your heart with who God says you are and truth from His word. It may not come overnight, but consistent application of the word to your mind will bring change.

THERE'S NO PLACE FOR SELF-PITY AND LIES ABOUT
UNWORTHINESS OR CRIPPLED ABILITIES WHEN YOU
FLOOD YOUR HEART WITH WHO GOD SAYS YOU ARE.

In what areas do you or your children play victim or indulge in self-pity? What truths can you speak over your hearts and declare out loud in order to rewrite these lies that have allowed you to justify these actions? Ask God to help reveal any lies that He desires to expose and remove in your children or yourself.

Finally, brothers and sisters, whatever is true, whatever is noble, whatever is right, whatever is pure, whatever is lovely, whatever is admirable—if anything is excellent or praiseworthy—think about such things. (Philippians 4:8 NIV)

Chapter 16

Anger

*B*efore I became a mother, I worked as an elementary school teacher. I absolutely loved that job. Sure, the early mornings, measly pay, and the smell of the cafeteria were all a little draining, but there was something so special about that career. As a kindergarten teacher, each day I was greeted by tiny, eager faces, sweet smiles, and big hugs. I saw my role as a vital part of their upbringing. I had the joy of getting to introduce them to new concepts and watching them flourish and grow throughout the year. I was able to take numbers or letters on a page and make them come alive to a child and watch the joy in their eyes when they came to full understanding.

I quickly learned that in order to be successful and to truly make a difference, I needed to do more than just stand at the front of the room and bark commands. To truly spark joy and a love for learning, I needed to connect with my students and find out what their needs were. There was one particular student whom I remember making those connections with. His name was Carson. Carson was a rowdy boy who had a reputation of getting into mischief and goofing off instead of following directions. He was what most teachers would see as a nuisance or troublemaker. However, I had a soft spot for that little man.

I decided I would invest in this boy and see if maybe all he needed was a little encouragement and someone who believed in him. Each day I took the time to get down on his level and slowly give him directions for the assignment after I had already given them to the class. I would praise him publicly for his efforts and small wins. When he was mischievous, I would bite my tongue and talk to him calmly, but firmly, while establishing boundaries.

I'd love to continue this story by saying that now little Carson is destined for an Ivy League university and that he credits me for his success throughout school. Honestly, I have no clue where he is or if he even remembers my name! I will say that throughout that year, I saw tiny changes. I saw glimmers of hope and tiny bits of encouragement that maybe my hard work was paying off.

Fast forward seven years, and I was suddenly a homeschooling mom of three, still wearing yesterday's clothes, who saw teaching and parenting as a chore and was too busy picking cheerios up off the floor and bouncing a toddler on my hip to stop and enjoy the process. I will say though: the cafeteria at home smelled a lot better.

I found myself barking commands all day. I wasn't taking the time to make connections and use each opportunity as a teachable moment. When my kids would misbehave, I'd bark back, "Stop already! If you do that again you're in your room for the rest of the evening." I found myself constantly correcting and threatening, and I couldn't stand the atmosphere in our home. It became an atmosphere of frustration, anger, and rash words.

So, I did what I always do when I'm desperately searching for the right solution for a problem. I Googled it. Then I realized that's never the right thing to do. So, I got out my Bible.

It's here I find peace in a solution that actually works. Looking at Jesus, we can see the perfect example of a father. Though He didn't have any biological children, He did have His disciples. Let's be honest: they were pretty immature and needy at times much like children, as are we, but here's what Jesus constantly does that I'm most impressed with. He spends His time on Earth constantly teaching. Not just barking commands of "do not, or else." He pours into those around Him and equips them for the days ahead.

Looking at Jesus inspires me to change the way I parent my own children because it isn't some new parenting trend or some psychologist's idea of what turns children into successful, kind adults. It's a parenting course from the headmaster.

LOOKING AT JESUS INSPIRES ME TO CHANGE THE WAY I PARENT MY OWN CHILDREN BECAUSE IT ISN'T SOME NEW PARENTING TREND OR SOME PSYCHOLOGIST'S IDEA OF WHAT TURNS CHILDREN INTO SUCCESSFUL, KIND ADULTS. IT'S A PARENTING COURSE FROM THE HEADMASTER..

So what does it look like when the Teacher comes into your house? It looks like the kind of connections Jesus had built with His disciples. It looks like stories, metaphors, and taking the time to speak *to* your children instead of just *at* them. It looks like hard work. It's easy to resort to barking commands or corrections. It's much harder to stop what you're doing, get down on their level, connect with their heart, and have a teachable moment through conversation.

When the siblings fight, it's much easier to say, "Stop fighting or I'll throw that toy away!" It's more challenging, but far more rewarding and impactful, to stop and say, "Kids put the toy down and look at me. What I see here is dishonor. You are treating each other rudely over a toy. This is not who we are as a family. We go out of our way to show love to each other. How can we fix this?"

Same problem, same ultimate goal, but one approach teaches and the other one scolds. One displays honor; the other displays anger. One approaches the problem; the other approaches the heart.

Listen, I get it. You're busy, mama. You can't be the perfectly patient mom every second of the day. We don't live in a *Leave It to Beaver* world, and we're all bound to make mistakes. We might holler at our five-year-old to chill out when what they really need is a hug and our full attention. We might also accuse our eight-year-old of lying, never stopping to hear the whole story and allowing God to show us their hearts. That's why there's grace. We can also ask God to give us strength, wisdom, and self-discipline for changing the way we communicate with our children.

I challenge you to start speaking James 1:19 over yourself. Write it on your mirror. Journal it in your planner, or wherever you will see it daily. Then watch it transform your attitude and communication as He shows you areas where you need His guidance and refining. As you do this, you'll become more aware of the triggers that cause you to lose your cool, and the moments where you have trouble taming your tongue.

What would walking in James 1:19 look like in your home? Where do you need help holding your tongue, opening your eyes and ears, and allowing God to speak through you?

My dear brothers and sisters, take note of this: Everyone should be quick to listen, slow to speak and slow to become angry. (James 1:19 NIV)

Chapter 17

Insecurities

I remember the moment clearly. It was swimsuit season of 2015. I was two-kids-in to this whole motherhood thing, and my body was starting to show the signs of stress from carrying tiny human beings from embryo to watermelon size. My skin was sagging where it had once been smooth, my face was rounder than it had been in my youth, and I had fresh tattoos in the form of purple stretch marks on my stomach. As I searched the bathing suit racks in the department store, I felt my heart sink. I was dreading the next hour of trying on suits, only to be disappointed by what I saw in the mirror and to leave defeated.

There was a time in motherhood when I was defined by this. My worth was tied up in an unattainable goal of having the same body after bearing children as I did in college. I realize even more now as I sit and type this out how ridiculous that was, and it makes me wonder how many of you are thinking the same about the image you're clinging to.

As I tried on bathing suits and fought back frustrated tears, I was overcome with inadequacy and self-pity. "Pity Party for One" in Dressing Room #3! I would love to say this was the moment Jesus came riding into the dressing room on a white horse, picking me up and giving me a "you're more than your dress size" chat. I was too busy wallowing in my sorrows for that. Rain check, Jesus?

Actually, it took years before I saw the stupidity in my lofty, yet shallow, standards for myself. I was so focused on my outward imperfections, that I was unable to catch a glimpse of the destruction taking place inside. Instead of gaining beauty, I was gaining unrefined insecurities which dulled my beautiful character and light.

It wasn't until I let God's word flood this area of my heart that I received the healing and change in vision I desperately needed. I needed to be reminded that God designed us to radiate Him from our inner beings; that His eyes don't scan over our flesh looking for something to be called beautiful or worthy. The longer we spend grasping at meaningless mental trophies of worldly beauty in order to gain approval or turn a head, the deeper our dissatisfaction will become, and we will quickly realize that this game of chase is nothing more than a temporary source of joy.

Don't believe this truth? Have you ever read the statistics on mental health and happiness for the most beautiful women in the world? I recently read that 68% of models have anxiety or depression and 76% have been exposed to drugs and alcohol on the job. That statistic alone is enough to convince me to lay down the idol of vanity.

I am not saying we throw out our makeup, ditch our gym memberships, and replace them with Snickers and stretchy pants, misconstruing the need for self-care. Not at all. Get dressed up, throw on a pair of heels, and give yourself a catcall as you look in the mirror. Live a healthy life-style and take care of your body. Draw on those eyebrows and recreate that smoky eye you saw on YouTube if you want to. But do it all because it stems from inward confidence, not to make up for a lack thereof.

No amount of makeup is ever going to cover up a mountain of insecurity and body-shaming lies. If you don't address the root of the issue, you'll never radiate on the outside.

One of my favorite Bible verses on this matter is Proverbs 31:30 (NIV): "Charm is deceptive, and beauty is fleeting, but a woman who fears the Lord is to be praised." According to the Merriam-Webster dictionary, fleeting means "passing swiftly" and deceptive means "tending or having power to cause someone to accept as true or valid what is false or invalid." I don't know about you, but I don't want to spend my time on, or gain my worth from, something that is quickly fading and completely false. If, instead, we choose to become women "clothed in strength and dignity"(Prov. 31:25) then our worth becomes defined by strength, meaning "the capacity of an object or substance to withstand great force or pressure" and dignity, meaning "the quality or state of being worthy, honored, or esteemed." And this my friend, is truly attractive.

One more quick thing about that beautiful after-baby-body of yours. Whether you birthed your children biologically or not, we all hold the markings of our children in one way or another—and we need to remember these are *blessings*. We are so fortunate to have the opportunity to hold children in our arms. I can't help but envision desolate women around the globe with empty arms and longing hearts, that would trade places with us in an instant. Those dark circles under your eyes mean that you had the privilege of holding and comforting that baby in the middle of the night. Your not-so-perfect perkies droop delightfully because you were able to nourish and sustain your children. Your body holds the story of a blessed mother whose jewels are her children.

YOUR BODY HOLDS THE STORY OF A BLESSED MOTHER
WHOSE JEWELS ARE HER CHILDREN.

Have you been throwing a Pity Party for One in Dressing Room #3 as well? Do you tug at your sides or grimace when you see your face in the mirror? It's time to let that go. Don't spend years allowing the enemy to spoon-feed you lies about your true worth. Go to the Father and allow Him to take off your cloak of insecurities and replace it with one of strength and dignity.

Today, ask God to show you the beauty He placed inside of you and begin to declare Proverbs 31 over your life.

Charm is deceptive, and beauty is fleeting; but a woman who fears the Lord is to be praised. (Proverbs 31:30 ESV)

The Fluff Dry

Like a salon blow-out after a walk in the rain. Va-va-voom!

Chapter 18

The Power of Your Prayers

S o how did that heavy-duty wash feel? Do you feel like you've broken off some chains and rewritten some of the lies you were telling yourself? I hope so.

Now that we've accomplished the cleansing that Jesus wanted to do in your life, let's let Him build you up and form you into a new creation. Let's let Him fluff your spirit and dry your tears, and let's start by letting Him reveal to you something extraordinary He's gifted you with.

I'm talking about something so incredibly magnificent and powerful about you that it's going to change your life and your family forever.

You have a superpower.

You have the power to bring change. You have the power to transform your entire family with nothing more than your words.

Yes!

Isn't this wonderful news? You might even be able to finally get your husband to put his laundry *in* the hamper for once. (Actually, probably not, but it's worth a shot.) Now wait: before you go commanding and nagging your family right out the door, I should tell you one thing. Your superpower words only work in one way—as prayers lifted towards the Father. In fact, they only hold power when the Lord holds your meager words in His mighty hands, and blows life upon them, commanding earthly situations to align with His promises and will for your life.

What? You're telling me that informing my husband that he's a jerk isn't going to bring a spirit of peace and love into his heart? Been there, done that. Nope, mama, that just isn't going to happen. However, when we take our concerns, frustrations, and desires to our Heavenly Father, it's then that real change begins.

When my husband and I were newlyweds, I was certain he needed some help, maybe even mothering, to turn his bad habits into better ones that lived up to my standards. I was determined to teach him how to become a better person, much like myself, and I was convinced all it was going to take was a little persuading and training. Ha! How ridiculous this all sounds to me now. I was, in my own opinion, almost flawless, and my husband was like an un-house-trained puppy who was going to take some work. He didn't wash the dishes right, he hung wet towels over the door, he was too opinionated, he yelled too much, he was too cocky, and the list went on. It's no wonder our first year of marriage was fit for a reality TV show. It seemed like every couple of months someone would be packing their things and threatening to go "home," also known as mom and dad's spare bedroom.

It was during this rocky season of marriage that I was given some of the best advice of my life. I had a sweet friend, a spiritual mother if you will, who told me I would never see change unless I hit my knees. She spoke life into a part of me that never existed before. She called out the prayer warrior in me.

I honestly don't know if I would have taken her advice so seriously had I not been in such a desperate time of my life. I was so ready for change, so ready for light at the end of the tunnel, that I drank her words like an infant drinks milk. To me, they weren't just nice words of encouragement; I needed those words of instruction for survival.

Over the next few months, I hit my knees like I never had before. I remember racing home from my job every day with an intensity and anticipation for a chance to sit before the Lord on the bedroom closet floor in our little apartment. I began to crave time in prayer. It was there that I found peace and hope.

It wasn't long after I started praying that I started to understand the full power of prayer. I began to realize that my words weren't just wishful utterings to an unconcerned God. They were words turned into missiles by a mighty hand, aimed at the wicked enemy of my soul. My prayers yielded to Jesus were used like a sharpened sword against the darkness. I prayed against my husband's temper, and it was smashed. I prayed that negative influences would vanish, and suddenly my husband got a new position away from the women I knew the Holy Spirit was leading me to pray protection against. I prayed he would be able to come to church with me, and without any reason, he was suddenly given Sunday mornings and Wednesday evenings off, which he was previously told was impossible.

I learned that when I aligned myself with Gods' word and His will for our lives, that my prayers were like turbo power in the vehicle to where God wanted us.

So, let me ask you, friend, how's your prayer life? I'm not sure if you have that spiritual mother in your life like I did, but would you let me be that for you? Would you let me speak those words of instruction and encouragement to you now?

James 5:16 (NIV), says this: "Therefore confess your sins to each other and pray for each other so that you may be healed. The prayer of a righteous person is powerful and effective." Powerful and effective. Your prayers are like Oxiclean to a grass-stained uniform, or like a Mr. Clean eraser to that artwork your four-year-old drew all over your wall. They are powerful and effective, friend. If you only look at that grass-stained uniform, simply wishing, hoping, and commanding it to be clean, you're not going to see any change. Likewise, if you do nothing more than look at your family while wishing, hoping, and telling them to change, well then you might as well take a seat and get comfortable. You're going to stay there a while.

> YOUR PRAYERS ARE LIKE OXICLEAN TO A GRASS-STAINED UNIFORM, OR A MR. CLEAN ERASER TO THAT ARTWORK YOUR FOUR-YEAR-OLD DREW ALL OVER YOUR WALL. THEY ARE POWERFUL AND EFFECTIVE.

You have a powerful shield and blade, friend. A full armor powered by Jesus—but it doesn't do any good if you never use it.

Since that first year of our marriage, I have probably spent entire days of my life on my knees. I've prayed for healing and seen miracles. I've prayed for bills to be paid and saw the exact dollar amount needed appear in our bank account. Yet, there are probably a thousand things I'm still praying for that I won't see come to fruition for decades. I pray for my kids' spouses. I pray for their friendships. I pray for generations to come, that they would choose to follow Jesus. I pray because it's a force that brings change like nothing else.

Are you ready for change in your life too? Ask the Lord today to begin to give you the discipline and hunger for time in His presence, interceding for your family. Ask the Lord to bring out the prayer warrior in you that He's longing to embrace. He's there waiting. Are you ready?

And I tell you, ask, and it will be given to you; seek, and you will find; knock, and it will be opened to you. (Luke 11:9 ESV)

Chapter 19

Praise During the Storm

Picture the scene. It's pouring down rain outside and you've been stuck in the house for the last six days straight with three kids under the age of six. At this point you've exhausted all indoor activities, including dressing up the cats, mattress surfing down the stairs, and a long game of hide and seek where you did all the counting and somehow always took about thirty-five minutes to actually find the children. (You did remember to wipe the chocolate off your face before finding them so your secret wouldn't be discovered, right?) Just before you're about to enforce early naptime at ninety-thirty a.m., your kids ask you if they can play outside.

You look at the rain pouring out the window. You look back at your newly mopped (okay, newly spot-cleaned with a baby wipe) floors and back at your children in their pajamas.

In this moment what do you do? Embrace your cool mom side and say "Absolutely! In fact, take my Pampered Chef pie pans and make mud pies while you're out there!"

Or do you instead tell them that you would gladly let them play outside in the rain, except that it's a known fact that children who play in the rain will get pneumonia and die?

I was a cool mom the other day. It doesn't happen often, and my baby-wipe-cleaned floors greatly suffered, but I learned something valuable as I watched them play. Standing in my doorway, as the rain gushed over the rooftop, I watched their little figures dancing through the raindrops, splashing in the puddles, and twirling underneath their umbrellas. One word kept coming to my mind. Joy. Complete, total, unexplainable joy.

In fact, this joy was so pure, so tangible, and so expressive, the pounding performance of the rain became a mere backdrop in the shadow of their exuberance. It was as if there was no rain at all, just children dancing joyfully. Children have a way of finding the beauty in the chaos, don't they?

They have a way of looking past the negatives, past the obstacles, and past anything that would prohibit them from turning a storm into a moment of joy. They don't see the rain as something sent to ruin their day and mess up their plans; they see the rain as an unexpected change of plans hiding a delightful gift.

This message struck my heart deeply that day, and reminded me of the storms I've been through in my life, including the day my career was pulled out from underneath me.

Before the days of cheerios in my bed and sippy cups in my sink, I was a working girl; a professional, bright-eyed, kindergarten teacher dreaming of all the years ahead I'd spend in my new career. I had worked so hard for that teaching degree, and was pleased with the steady income I was finally earning post-graduation. My husband was working in parks and recreation at the time, and between the two of us, we were able to cover the bills and have a little left over for dinner dates and new clothes. Life was perfect, in our young, tunnel-vision eyes.

Then came a day that absolutely blindsided me. Shortly after deciding to start our family, I waddled into my principal's office, carrying the weight of a third trimester belly, for our end of the year review. As I waited in anticipation to hear what grade I would be assigned to the following year, my principal praised me for my hard work and dedication. I beamed and soaked up each and every compliment, all the way up until I begin to feel the conversation shift. Suddenly, he was no longer smiling and his tone was solemn. He informed me about all the recent budget cuts and teacher layoffs, and before I knew it, I found myself sitting in his chair as an unemployed, pregnant twenty-five-year-old.

My security, my plan, and my career had all been stripped away in an instant. After going home to inform my husband, pouting over a pint of ice cream, and generating plans on how to hide a nine-month belly in teaching interviews, my husband and I decided that we'd just figure it out and somehow learn to live on his income. Fast forward six months, and this newlywed couple and new baby were living with her parents in order to get out of debt and afford groceries.

This is when I learned that our storms, or sudden change in plans, don't surprise God at all. As I sat stunned in my principal's chair that day, Jesus was right behind me telling me it would be okay, because He had a greater plan. After living with my parents for two years, we were out of debt and purchasing our first home, my husband had a new, higher paying job, and I was living out my dream of being a stay-at-home mom. Had we stayed complacent in our previous careers, we would have missed the life-changing opportunity God had waiting for us.

If we can learn to trust God without reservation and praise Him in the middle of hardship, focusing instead on the work taking place in our hearts and the blessing on the other side of the pain, we'll begin to see these difficulties as glorious opportunities to watch the hand of God in our lives.

So, what's the weather like at your house? Is it raining there too, friend?

Has life sent a storm that has you retreating indoors, hiding away, sulking, grieving, or complaining? Maybe it's a hard week of parenting, a crummy job, a strained relationship, or something else that just has you worn out.

We have a choice in life: we can choose to let our situations rule our attitudes, or we can let attitudes rule our situations. We can choose to allow the rain to make our hearts bitter, or we can allow the rain to draw out an exquisite presentation of thankfulness and worship to be used for the glory of the Most High. God's divine purpose in allowing us to weather the storm is not to stir up bitterness and harden hearts, it's to cultivate a steadfast spirit of praise within us that can withstand winds of shattering strength, so that we may be a light to a dejected world.

> WE HAVE A CHOICE IN LIFE: WE CAN CHOOSE TO LET OUR SITUATIONS RULE OUR ATTITUDES, OR WE CAN LET ATTITUDES RULE OUR SITUATIONS.

If you can't think of anything to be thankful for, start with this thought: if we never went through battles, never had struggles, we'd have no need for a savior. We would never grow in our faith, get rid of our inadequacies, and be elevated to a greater place in Him. We'd be stagnant, complacent, and content with the mundane. He'd never be able to use us to pull others out of the trenches who are trudging through similar struggles. We'd never find true fulfillment. Now isn't that reason enough for praise? He cares about us too much to keep us stagnant and stunted. His word says in Romans 5:3-4 (NIV), "Not only so, but we also glory in our sufferings, because we know that suffering produces perseverance, perseverance, character; and character, hope."

Just like our children take an ominous, bone-chilling rainstorm and turn it into a jubilant adventure, we have the ability to take our gloomiest moments in life and turn them into something beautiful, memorable, and something to be captivated by—something to be used for His glory.

What can you be thankful for today, friend? Ask God to give you the strength to praise Him during the storm, so that your actions set a powerful example of faith and trust for your children to see.

And the God of all grace, who called you to his eternal glory in Christ, after you have suffered a little while, will himself restore you and make you strong, firm and steadfast. (1 Peter 5:10 NIV)

Chapter 20

Heavenly Perspective

Seven years ago, I made the decision to homeschool my children. With lots of time spent in prayer, knowing that God had called me to this journey, I was eagerly looking forward to the days ahead of exploring, educating, and enjoying those precious moments with my children.

I saw my homeschool journey like a pastel watercolor canvas painting of a mother holding her children in her arms, while reading *Little House On the Prairie*. Let me go back and edit that picture just a bit to reflect the reality. What I didn't realize is that I'd be nursing the baby in one arm to keep her from making noise, trying to hold the book in the other hand, stopping every thirty-three seconds to tell the four-year-old to stop singing *Beauty and the Beast* overtop of mommy while she's reading, and promising the seven-year-old we would indeed finish the book before she graduates high school.

The truth is homeschooling is really, really hard sometimes. It is so easy to get bogged down with feelings of inadequacy, or with the tasks we *think* we need to cross off the list in order for our children to be successful. For our children, the same is true. School is a long journey that takes thousands of small steps added together, hundreds of small disciplines built upon each other, and countless hours spent practicing skills to come to the grand finale of a diploma or degree. Try telling a seven-year-old this though, and you might as well go ahead and cut the cheese and get out the grapes to go with all the whine you'll be consuming.

With my oldest daughter, I've found that focusing on all the steps along the way to any big goal is just too much for her. Take reading for example. Reading didn't come easy for her and it was far from her favorite subject. Schooling her on all of the many sounds each letter makes and slogging through word deciphering alongside her was always a battle. There were just too many rules, and so many items to memorize. It was taxing and felt like a chore for both of us.

We struggled through this for about a year until I finally grasped ahold of the life-changing concept I'm about to share with you. I was focusing so much on showing her the "steps" of reading that I was neglecting to show her the reward. I failed to immerse her in the brilliant pleasure of simply *listening* in anticipation to dynamic plots unfolding, as girls became warriors, horses became friends, or peasants became royalty. I failed to offer her a preview of the delight she would experience in a well-told story.

In my quiet time just the other morning, as I lifted up my children in prayer, God began to speak to me about shifting my focus and exposing my children to a glimpse of the great reward we have as Christians. It's so easy to set our children's focus on their feet, emphasizing the daily steps we take; all the biblical principles and verses they need to take to heart and the narrow path they're called to walk on. God showed me that while we might have great intentions in ensuring our children play the part, if we don't spend more time turning their focus to the great reward, we are missing the biggest component.

Why do we walk the narrow path? Why do we spend our lives loving our neighbor as ourselves? Why do we spend time in God's presence, getting to know His heart? Because at the end of all of this is the most beautiful place we will ever see, with a God full of more love than we have ever experienced. When we grasp hold of the reward and the end-goal, taking the steps becomes a joy.

Later that morning, my kids and I spent some time talking about what we thought Heaven would be like and what we would be most excited about. Some of the things were silly, like "all-you-can-eat ice cream" or "a house full of baby kittens of every color" but there were also moments where they mentioned getting to hug Jesus or see God and it encouraged my spirit to know that they were grasping it. They were fixing their eyes on the great reward.

Maybe you feel like me and are wondering if you're fitting it all in. Maybe you're wondering if you're giving your children a solid enough foundation so they won't stray from God as they get older. Take rest in this, my friend. Show them Jesus. Show them what He promises for us in Heaven. Show them the love we will come face-to-face with for eternity, so that as they walk the narrow path, their eyes will be fixed on the reward and not their feet.

SHOW THEM THE LOVE WE WILL COME FACE-TO-FACE WITH FOR ETERNITY, SO THAT AS THEY WALK THE NARROW PATH, THEIR EYES WILL BE FIXED ON THE REWARD AND NOT THEIR FEET.

Colossians 3:2 says, "Set your minds on things that are above, not on things that are on earth." God knows us well. He knows that if our eyes were to stray from the ultimate, unfailing gift of eternal life with Him, our actions would become empty and meaningless, and we'd quickly be swallowed by earthly hardships, losing our hope in Him. The things of the earth are temporary, unsatisfying, discouraging, difficult, and sometimes painful. However, the things of Heaven are life-giving, without burden, joyous, and encouraging, and when we set our mind on these things, it makes the journey much easier.

Do you find yourself wondering if your children are fully grasping the big picture of life with Jesus? Ask God today to teach you and your children about Heaven and how our purpose here on earth fits into that. Pray God will give you a desire to know Him and what He has for us.

Brothers and sisters, I do not consider myself yet to have taken hold of it. But one thing I do: Forgetting what is behind and straining toward what is ahead, I press on toward the goal to win the prize for which God has called me heavenward in Christ Jesus. (Phillipians 3:13 NIV)

Chapter 21

Redefining Your View of Jesus

If you ask any five-year-old to describe Santa Clause, you'll likely get answers all landing in the same general description: jolly, plump, happy, kind. Ask any child to list the qualities of Superman and again, you'll get brave, strong, or lightning fast. Ask those same children to tell you about the character of God, and you'll suddenly find a vast difference in answers.

For some He is brave, strong, mighty, but distant and uninvolved. For others, He is kind, gentle, patient, and a close friend. Yet still for some He is cold, hard, judgmental, and angry. Why are the answers so scattered when it comes to defining the Creator of the universe when we can so quickly and accurately identify a superhero or fictional character?

Here's why: because we often directly correlate the attributes of our Heavenly Father to the attributes of our earthly father. When our earthly father is distant, critical, and unloving, we see God as a judgmental ruler, looking down from Heaven, waiting for us to make our next mistake so He can punish us. When our earthly father is a provider and a hard worker, but lacks any relationship with us, we see the act of approaching God in prayer as a nuisance, and we don't believe He desires to live in relationship with us.

When our oldest daughter was around the age of three, my husband decided to start the tradition of taking her on daddy-daughter dates. He would get dressed up and she would get to pick the restaurant, and the two of them would spend the evening together doing whatever it was that brought her joy. They would go see a movie, feed ducks at the pond, or just do a puzzle together at home. He has continued this tradition with all of our girls; the reason behind it being he wants our girls to experience what it's like to be treated kindly and respectfully by a man, so they will have the same expectations for a spouse. His reasoning and efforts touch my heart so deeply, but I also see something else happening in those little hearts. Every time he pursues that relationship with them, he's giving them a taste of the relationship God desires to have with them.

What was your relationship with your father like? Some of us are blessed to have present fathers in our lives who have exemplified kindness, patience, and a deep love. Then there are some of us who didn't even have a chance to experience that because our earthly fathers never stuck around. Or maybe our fathers *did* stick around but the physical or mental pain they caused makes us wish they hadn't. I don't know your story, friend, what you've been through or been spared from, but of one thing I am sure. We serve the same God.

The same loving, powerful, intentional, relational father who catches my tears, holds no records of my wrongs, and gives me peace when I need it most, is the exact same God for you.

THE SAME LOVING, POWERFUL, INTENTIONAL, RELATIONAL FATHER WHO CATCHES MY TEARS, HOLDS NO RECORDS OF MY WRONGS, AND GIVES ME PEACE WHEN I NEED IT MOST, IS THE EXACT SAME GOD FOR YOU.

Do you have a hard time believing that? Does it look good on paper for you, but when you pray you're flooded with painful reminders of your earthly Father? Or do you long for that deep, intense connection with Him, but can't seem to cross the canyon you feel lies between?

There is good news for all of us no matter what our experience here on earth has been. There is a remedy for our skewed view of God, and that comes through reading the truth.

Every unfitting view of the Father can be corrected when you look in His word. In John 14:7 (NIV), Jesus says, "If you really know me, you will know my father as well. From now on you do know him and have seen him."

When we want to study the nature of God, we can look at Jesus. Who was He? Isaiah 9:6 (NIV) says, "For to us a child is born, to us a son is given, and the government will be on his shoulders. And he will be called Wonderful Counselor, Mighty God, Everlasting Father, Prince of Peace." I don't know about you, but this sounds like exactly what I need in my life. Someone to help guide my steps, someone to do the miraculous, and someone to bring peace in the middle of the circus I call home.

If you're struggling with buying into committing daily time to Jesus, let me encourage you to allow God to show you who He truly is. By soaking in His presence, and immersing ourselves in scripture, we move towards His heart. Every time we do this, our character begins to sharpen, because like a good father, He's not going to let us stay broken. He gently reveals the hurts, lack of trust, unforgiveness, and anger. We begin to know Him, trust Him, and look like Him. Once you get a taste, sweet mama, you'll never want to go back. We need Him so desperately in our homes, and our children need to see the example of this ongoing friendship. Will you allow Him to rewrite your definition of who He is today?

The Lord is gracious and righteous; our God is full of compassion. (Psalm 116:5 NIV)

Chapter 22

Nearsightedness

*E*ver since I was in the fifth grade, I have worn either glasses or contacts. I distinctly remember the moment I discovered my vision was off. My mom was standing in the kitchen holding up a box of cereal asking, "Can you read this?"

A week later I was sitting in the eye doctor's office being fitted for my first pair of glasses to correct my nearsighted vision. As I have aged, unfortunately, my vision has worsened and my prescription has only increased. I'm pretty sure my college years of burning the candle at both ends of the wick probably took me on an expedited path through vision weakening. In fact, now if I am without my glasses, I likely won't even know it's a box of cereal at all!

What I have found with my nearsightedness is that I'm unable to see anything beyond my nearest surroundings. I can clearly see the chair I'm sitting on, and the little one at my feet. My husband across the room? He's just a blur. If I were to drive without glasses, I would only be able to see the car in front of me, not what lies on the road ahead. (Just to put your mind at ease, I do not drive without my contacts or glasses on!)

You know something? I've always felt like my visual eyes aren't the only part of me that's nearsighted.

We have other eyes outside of the ones which see colors, shapes, faces, and depth. We have a set of eyes within our spirit; eyes that see our road ahead and the vision for our future. These "spirit eyes" of mine tend to have the same nearsighted handicap as my physical eyes.

When my oldest daughter was about to turn two, we began the daunting task of potty training. (Yes, I was way more ambitious with my first child. Ask me at what age I plan on starting with my third and you'll get a totally different answer.) When we started, I decided we would just dive headfirst into this potty-training world and would ace it in a few days.

Go ahead and laugh. I'm sure laughing at myself now!

It took months of holding my breath as we braved the world outside our home, racing down grocery store aisles, darting through theme park walkways, or fleeing the social circle at gatherings in a rush for the bathroom before she finally started to get it. It wasn't until she turned three that she was fully trained at night as well. I was starting to feel like it would never end.

When you're in the middle of a tiring season or phase with your kids it's easy to become nearsighted. It's easy to lose sight of the long-term goals and the outcome of your hard work. In the middle of training my two-year-old I couldn't see the finish line. All I could do was focus on the next twenty minutes and whether or not she was going to wet her pants while sitting on grandma's lap. I couldn't help but feel like we were taking one step forward only to take two steps back.

While my kids are not yet grown and we are still in the "laundry years," I have a sneaking suspicion that this nearsighted tendency isn't going to end anytime soon. The things we do over and over and over again every day will be the things that slowly build these little hearts into mighty men and women of God. But we can't see this on our own.

When I was ten years old being examined by the eye doctor, he already knew I couldn't see without help. He knew it would take the strength of those prescription glasses to transform my vision from being able to see three feet to thirty feet. I would have to rely on the strength of something that could compensate for my weakness.

We all need those glasses, friend. Without God's heavenly view of our lives, our calling, and our future, we all walk around in a state of limited vision. We are imperfect, impatient, and incapable of understanding how our little steps add up to His big picture. That's why we need to ask Him for a set of new eyes.

One of the most impactful points of my marriage came when I simply asked God to give me His eyes to see my marriage. We had just been through an extremely challenging time and I was left wondering how I'd have vision for the future. Do you know what? He did exactly that. I suddenly saw how everything we had been through was pointing towards something greater.

When you get the grand vision for your journey in motherhood, it's easier to aim for the mark, and keep pushing through.

WHEN YOU GET THE GRAND VISION FOR YOUR
JOURNEY IN MOTHERHOOD, IT'S EASIER TO AIM FOR
THE MARK, AND KEEP PUSHING THROUGH.

Will you ask God to do the same for your journey? Ask Him to give you His eyes to see your children, and your role as their mother. Ask Him to show you the payoff to all the sleepless nights, tantrum tackling, and dinner preparations. Just like a child putting on a pair of glasses for the first time, you'll be delighted at how much clearer and more enjoyable your walk becomes.

Having the eyes of your hearts enlightened, that you may know what is the hope to which he has called you, what are the riches of his glorious inheritance in the saints. (Ephesians 1:18 ESV)

Chapter 23

Living For Him

"Mom, can you help me find my Barbie?" I hear from the other room.

"Just a minute, sweetie. I just have to finish sending this message," I reply.

"Mommy! You told me you would read this book to me and I'm still waiting!"

"Okay! Just one more minute, I promise."

"Moooommmmyy! Sissy is climbing on top of the table! She opened your permanent markers, and is coloring on her head!"

Yep. That'll do it. "You've got my attention, kids."

There are two different kinds of minutes in this world. A standard minute measured by seconds, and a mom-minute measured by urgency of the task, length of current to-do list, and mental state of the mom. One should never confuse the two, as a "mom minute" very rarely is ever actually sixty seconds or less. Not even by a long shot.

In those mom minutes of my day, I often hear myself saying that same phrase over and over again: "Just a minute." Recently it's become more painfully obvious than ever how often I push my kids to the back burner to get one more task done. I just need to send one more message, do one more batch of laundry, or finish scrubbing my baseboards—okay fine, I haven't actually cleaned my baseboards once in the last two years. However, I have done my share of laundry, messaging, and staring at a screen instead of their little faces. I have a feeling I'm not alone in this.

There is a war we fight today as parents unlike any other fight in generations past. Today we fight for time. We fight for intentionality. We fight for being present. If we aren't careful, we'll lose that fight and will look back wondering where all the years went and why we don't feel as connected to our children as we should.

Now this does not mean that we ignore the house, say goodbye to the outside world, and spend all our free time playing hide-and-seek and reading Winnie the Pooh. Absolutely not. It also doesn't mean you have to quit your job, or feel like there's no hope because you're a single working mom. That's all mommy guilt, and we covered that earlier.

All this means is we have to learn to be wise stewards of the time we *do* have. I don't care if it's twelve hours or twelve minutes a day. The amount of intentionality with which you spend your time is far more important than the amount of time you're given to be intentional with. You might only get to see your children for one hour a day, and that could easily be more impactful than a mom who spends sunrise to sunset with hers but barely has a meaningful conversation. Presence isn't enough.

THE AMOUNT OF INTENTIONALITY WITH WHICH YOU SPEND YOUR TIME IS FAR MORE IMPORTANT THAN THE AMOUNT OF TIME YOU'RE GIVEN TO BE INTENTIONAL WITH.

So how do we make sure we are stewarding our time well?

In Psalms 90:12 (ESV), Moses cries out to God, "So teach us to number our days, that we may get a heart of wisdom." What does this mean? This means that when we have an eternal view of life here on earth—a view of our purpose in relation to the small amount of time we are granted—we begin to spend our time wisely and selflessly. We begin to see our days as mini-missions that all point towards a grand finish.

Imagine you are given an extremely time-consuming assignment from a college professor. After he outlines in great detail exactly what he expects, he adds that this project will determine your final grade—and that it's due in just three days. Now imagine yourself walking home pondering the weight of this project and brainstorming how you will accomplish it. As you walk in the door, realizing the time clock for this assignment started ticking immediately, how will you spend the next three days? Will you sit down, turn on the TV, and veg out? Probably not. It's very unlikely you'd be thinking about wasting time on anything other than that project for every hour of the next three days.

What if we learned to look at this life as a grand, God-glorifying, magnificent assignment given to us from our Heavenly Father? What if we looked at our days as ticking seconds in the thrilling race to the finish? Would we spend our days differently? Less time with the repetitive, unfruitful tasks that pull us away from the meaningful, life-giving opportunities? Would we sit and have face-to-face conversations with our children at dinner instead of turning on the TV? Would we fight the urge to "check out" on our phones and be present with our families, knowing that this time spent is depositing money into their lifelong banks? Would we let the laundry linger a little longer in the hamper to pull our children on our laps and read them a story?

As soon as we understand this life has nothing to do with us and has everything to do with the One who even allowed us to be here, we can begin to live intentionally and make our moments, hours, or minutes truly matter. It's then that we'll see our days as opportunities to participate in His grand plan.

Today ask God to show you the opportunities to love, share, encourage, nurture, teach, guide, forgive, and bring glory to His name with all your moments.

Look carefully then how you walk, not as unwise but as wise, making the best use of the time, because the days are evil. Therefore do not be foolish, but understand what the will of the Lord is. (Ephesians 5:15-17 ESV)

Chapter 24

Undeserved Grace

*J*ust the other day, my middle child stood just outside the open sliding glass door at the back of our house. The kids had been playing outside and making mud pies, and she was standing there with a huge smile on her face, gazing up at a frog perched above the door. In her hand was a giant fistful of homemade mud ready to take its flight towards the poor, unsuspecting frog. I saw her wind up her arm and take aim, but in my head, I was thinking, "Surely not. Surely she knows better than to throw mud directly at the open door."

I was wrong. Apparently, there was no red flag, warning signal, or even a small thought of "this might not be a good idea." With full force and all the joy in the world, she proceeded to fling a mound of mud straight through our sliding glass door into the kitchen, where it scattered and smeared all over the table, chairs, and floor.

I had no words. I believe my mouth may have just dropped open; my eyes wider than a deer in a staring contest. My kids stared back. I could tell they were waiting to see if steam was about to start rolling out of my ears and if my voice would transform into The Hulk. I looked at my middle child's sweet little face and saw the realization of what she had just done. All the joy was gone and now she was waiting to see what the consequences of her actions might be. She stepped back, sunk into her shoulders, and put her hand up on her mouth. Guilt had just gripped her heart, and it was clear to me she was just as surprised by her actions as I was.

In this moment, I had a choice. I could choose to continue to rub her face in the mistake she had just made, or I could jump on the opportunity to show her just what the Father's love and grace looks like. After a moment, I let out a laugh. The kids, looking at each other to confirm this really was happening, began to laugh with me. We sat there for a good couple of minutes reliving the unexpected dirt shower and giggling about what must have been going through her mind as she watched it land all over the kitchen. Then I hugged her and told her that I forgave her, as I handed her a broom to clean it up.

There's something we can all learn from this image of my sweet four-year-old. You see, we are just like her. All of us. We are children of God, trying to do our best on earth, but often falling short of the mark. We get caught up in our emotions, be it joy, sadness, or anger, and we make impulsive decisions that have consequences. Oftentimes, it's in that same moment that we feel the immediate weight of the guilt and conviction, and if our heart is soft, we turn to the Father.

If we served a Father who was full of fury and wrath, we'd get immediate lashing and humiliation, but we don't. How blessed are we to have a God full of mercy and grace? When our hearts are in a state of repentance, He is quick to forgive, and while we may still have a mess to clean up, guilt and shame don't stay smeared across our hearts like the mud on my kitchen floor. 1 John 1:9 says, "If we confess our sins, he is faithful and just to forgive us our sins and to cleanse us from all unrighteousness."

HE IS QUICK TO FORGIVE, AND WHILE WE MAY STILL
HAVE A MESS TO CLEAN UP, GUILT AND SHAME DON'T
STAY SMEARED ACROSS OUR HEARTS LIKE THE MUD ON
MY KITCHEN FLOOR.

Being able to show our children what grace looks like in a tangible way is a beautiful thing. They need to see what it looks like when someone deserves the ultimate penalty but gets redemption, love, and forgiveness instead. We all deserved death. We all deserved a black mark on our book for all the things we did wrong. Instead we got eternal life. Instead we got a love greater than anything we will ever experience. Instead we got a Savior whose blood wiped away every black mark in our book for all of eternity.

Our kids need to know this exists. They need to know there's a place they can lay down their shortcomings and find comfort and forgiveness. We can't always forgo the consequences and laugh at the situation, but we can choose to always bring them back to repentance and forgiveness.

Today, ask God to give you a fresh perspective of His grace and how to display that for your children.

Who is a God like you, who pardons sin and forgives the transgression of the remnant of his inheritance? You do not stay angry forever but delight to show mercy. You will again have compassion on us; you will tread our sins underfoot and hurl all our iniquities into the depths of the sea. (Micah 7:18-19 NIV)

Final Thoughts

*oday as I parented my three children, swept my dirty floors, and cooked what seemed like fifteen meals, I thought of you. I thought of the arduous struggles we both go through as mothers, and the moments of defeat, exhaustion, and heartache we share. I thought of the nights we both sit there, face in a bowl of ice cream, trying to recover from the whirlwind of the day. We need each other.

Truth is, even if you write an entire book on finding your joy and purpose in motherhood, you will still have days where the enemy's sneaky attacks get the best of you. No matter how many times you've told yourself to give it all to God, you'll still have days where you need a reminder of His unyielding faithfulness when your flesh rises up against your spirit.

Know that you are normal.

Do me a favor. Don't put this book away and let it collect dust in the forgotten section of your closet. Use it as a tool. When you find yourself drowning in mommy guilt, open the worn pages of this book and reread the verses and stories your spirit needs that day. When a catastrophic storm sweeps through your life, flip to the chapter that reminds you to praise Him and equips you with verses to declare. Let me be the friend on your bookshelf who points you back to Jesus on your hardest days.

Mothering is hard, but mothering has a purpose greater than any other calling on this earth. You, my friend, are chosen for this very purpose. When you begin to see your daily grind as opportunities for Jesus to shape you, maybe you also will find those lessons in the laundry basket.

Works Cited

Merriam-Webster Online, s.v. "Fleeting," accessed June 1, 2019, https://www.merriam-webster.com/dictionary/fleeting.

Merriam-Webster Online, s.v. "Deceptive," accessed June 1, 2019, https://www.merriam-webster.com/dictionary/deceptive.

Merriam-Webster Online, s.v. "Strength," accessed June 1, 2019, https://www.merriam-webster.com/dictionary/strength.

Merriam-Webster Online, s.v. "Dignity," accessed June 1, 2019, https://www.merriam-webster.com/dictionary/dignity.

"Reports." The Model Alliance. Accessed June 1, 2019. https://modelalliance.org/industry-analysis.

CPSIA information can be obtained
at www.ICGtesting.com
Printed in the USA
LVHW021518100222
710326LV00007B/85